THE TEN THOUSAND LEAVES

IAN HIDEO LEVY

The Ten Thousand Leaves

A TRANSLATION OF THE
Man'yōshū,
JAPAN'S PREMIER
ANTHOLOGY OF
CLASSICAL POETRY

VOLUME ONE

PRINCETON UNIVERSITY PRESS

Copyright © 1981 by Princeton University Press
Published by Princeton University Press, Princeton, New Jersey
In the United Kingdom:
Princeton University Press, Guildford, Surrey

All Rights Reserved

ISBN 0-691-00029-8 (pbk.)

First Princeton Paperback printing, 1987

This book has been composed in Linotron Sabon

Clothbound editions of Princeton University Press books
are printed on acid-free paper, and binding materials
are chosen for strength and durability. Paperbacks, while satisfactory
for personal collections, are not usually suitable for library rebinding.

Printed in the United States of America by
Princeton University Press, Princeton, New Jersey

For My Parents

CONTENTS

THE TEN THOUSAND LEAVES

INTRODUCTION

The Ten Thousand Leaves is Japan's first anthology of poetry and, to over a millennium of critical opinion, the greatest. Like the works of Homer for the West, like *The Book of Songs* for China, it represents both the classical fount of poetry and a model of expressive energy never surpassed.

As its name—*Man'yōshū*, literally "the collection of ten thousand leaves"—suggests, this is the "anthology of all anthologies" from the Asuka and Nara periods, which saw the first flowering of an artistic and literary sensibility in Japan. Apart from a few poems attributed to legendary times, and some others which may possibly be additions from as late as the ninth century, *The Ten Thousand Leaves* is a collection of poetry written from the second quarter of the seventh century to the middle of the eighth. The last specifically dated poem was composed in 759.

The Ten Thousand Leaves is a vast work, comprising 4,516 poems in twenty "books" (*maki*, or "scrolls"). In them are represented over 400 named poets, and countless hundreds of others who composed the anonymous poems which make up more than half of the collection. The variety is astonishing, ranging from the elegant banquet verse of aristocrats to the "poems of the frontier guardsmen" and the rustic "poems of the Eastland" in provincial dialect.

It is difficult to characterize *The Ten Thousand Leaves* as a whole, although many have tried. Some have spoken of it as a work of simple clarity, mainly in contrast to the sophisticated word play which is often such an important element in later Japanese poetry. Yet it includes poems of great length and structural intricacy, expressing a purely lyrical impulse—almost entirely free of discursive abstraction—on a scale rarely found in Western poetry. Some stress the fact that *The Ten Thousand Leaves* preserves a "pure" japanese voice at a time of enthusiastic borrowing from China and Korea. Yet the mix of Chinese characters used semantically and phonetically in *The Ten Thousand Leaves* is strikingly similar to the script used in recording Korean poetry at the time, and the collection includes several Confucian and Taoist expositions, written entirely in Chinese, among poems which seem to come straight out of primitive Shinto.

The Ten Thousand Leaves is, above all, a *representative* work, a culling of many different styles of verbal expression from a period of dramatic cultural growth parallelled in Japanese history perhaps only by the last hundred years. The seventh and eighth centuries saw the first attempts to create a national entity, centered on a political cult of the Emperor, out of the archaic coalition of clans which "Japan" had been. They witnessed the birth of Japanese art in that Buddhist sculpture and architecture which reveals, in the tapered lines of Bodhisattva torsos and the entasis of temple pillars, a distant Greek inspiration, reborn in wood and painted in the colors of a new faith accrued in its millennial journey across the Asian continent. And surely the most remarkable development of this time was the rise of an urban civilization literally out of the rice paddies—the Fujiwara capital of the 690's, Japan's first large-scale "city," and the great capital at Nara, founded in 710 and laid out in broad symmetrical avenues that stretched across the northern arc of the Yamato basin in a reach for the grandeur of T'ang China.

But *The Ten Thousand Leaves* is its own monument. The number of liturgical "Buddhist poems" in the collection —from an age in which the nation's treasure was poured into the construction of the Great Buddha at the Tōdaiji temple—can be counted on one hand. The civilization of Asuka and Nara did not use its native verse to commemorate its achievements in other fields, but allowed it to grow in its own indigenous directions *as poetry*. Thus, for example, even as the Japanese grew adept at writing historical prose studded with the most sophisticated Chinese rhetorical embellishments, a poet like Kakinomoto Hitomaro could write a lengthy war scene (in II. 199) whose *conception* owes much to the Chinese Histories, yet write it entirely in Japanese verse, one hypotactic sentence rich with inflections and original metaphors—and without a single Chinese word.

The Ten Thousand Leaves is a chorus of lyrical voices born from out of a tradition of ritual verbal art that stretches back into Japan's pre-literate centuries, back into myth itself. The earliest poems in the collection are similar to many of the folk poems recorded in Japan's oldest books, those melanges of history and myth called the *Kojiki* ("The Record of Ancient Matters," 712) and the *Nihonshoki* ("The Records of Japan," 720). Like the archaic songs, they are built around expressions in the collective voice and eternal time of the ritual. *The Ten Thousand Leaves* opens with a poem attributed to Emperor Yūryaku (the traditional dates of his reign are 456-479). It begins with an amatory appeal:

> Girl with your basket,
>   with your pretty basket,
> with your shovel,
>   your pretty shovel,
> gathering shoots on the hillside here,
> I want to ask your home.
> Tell me your name!

Then what apparently was originally a folk poem, re-written for the imperial speaker, climaxes with the Emperor's statement of his identity with the land:

> This land of Yamato,
>   seen by the gods on high—
> it is all my realm,
> in all of it I am supreme.
> I will tell you
> my home and my name.

This is a mythic statement, the imprint in language of the collective existence of the clan, not the lovesong of an individual man. Similarly, when the Emperor Jomei (reigned 629-642) climbs to the summit of Kagu Hill, his view of his realm (I.2) is not a literal survey of the actual fields below but an eternal vision of ritual symmetry, in which

> On the plain of land,
> smoke from the hearths rises, rises.
>   On the plain of waters,
> gulls rise one after another.

After this couplet, which seems to be molded both by the example of the imagistic parallel couplet in Chinese Six Dynasties verse and by a native ritual division of the earth into its dual bounties of land and sea (which overrides the literal fact that there are neither sea nor gulls in inland Yamato), the Emperor concludes with ceremonial praise:

> A splendid land
>   is the dragonfly island,
> the land of Yamato.

Yamato, the land of these Emperors, is the rich, fertile basin in western Honshu where Japan's civilization was born. Its name seems to have the etymological implication of "the place between the mountains." Many poems in *The Ten Thousand Leaves* refer to the fact that Yamato could be entered or left only by crossing the surrounding mountains. With very few exceptions, the early Japanese Court was located on various sites within and around the Asuka valley, tucked in the southeastern corner of the Yamato Basin. The palace was rebuilt on a new site following the decease of an Emperor (in order to avoid the pollution of death), but the new site was almost always kept in or near Asuka until 710, when the capital was transferred to Nara in northern Yamato.

The sense of the sacredness of Yamato may be traced to the common mythic birth of the land and its ancestral inhabitants, as recorded in the animistic genealogy of the *Kojiki* and the *Nihonshoki*. It is this animistic sensibility which lies behind the patterned, ritual evocations of the land in early poetry. Here are statements of an unchanging, and essentially religious, truth that exists in the collective mind of the clan. It is the Emperor's function as chief ritualist to pronounce it.

But already in the 640's, no more than a few years after Emperor Jomei's vision of Yamato's splendor in its eternal dual symmetry, we find the beginnings of a different kind of poetic statement, one in which a unique event in a specific, real time is recaptured in the memory of a poet composing as an individual. Princess Nukada, relating an imperial excursion, writes:

> I remember
> our temporary shelter
> by Uji's palace ground,
> when we cut the splendid grass
>   from the autumn fields
> and sojourned under thatch.   (I.7)

Here, in place of the "preestablished harmony" of ritual in a realm outside the ordinary bounds of time, is a procession of memory through its constituent images, details which are chosen by the poet's aesthetic consciousness from her own past experience. We know almost nothing about this woman who was Japan's first lyric poet. She may have been of Korean origin (as a good number of the Japanese cultural elite apparently were at this time), and she certainly was a central figure in the poetry circle which flourished during the reign of Emperor Tenji (661-671). Tenji was an enthusiastic student of Chinese literature under whose patronage continental scholars came to teach at the Japanese Court, armed with copies of the great Chinese anthology of poetry and prose, the *Wen Hsuan*.

One result was the beginning of *kanshi*, poetry written by the Japanese in the Chinese language. The preface to the *Kaifūsō* (751), the first anthology of *kanshi*, tells us that Emperor Tenji "from time to time invited men of literature to Court, and held banquets with sweet wine," that on these occasions "the Sovereign himself wrote literature, and his wise Ministers wrote odes of praise," and that "the phrases they carved and the beautiful tracings of their brushes exceeded a mere hundred."

Most of what the Japanese Court actually wrote in Chinese sounds derivative and stilted today. But far more important than their actual compositions in the foreign verse is the fact that the stimulation of this contact with Chinese literature seems to have given birth to a consciousness of verbal expression as a specifically aesthetic, rather than ritual, medium, and that this consciousness was applied to writing in Japanese as well. The result is most apparent in Princess Nukada's work from this period, especially her renowned poem comparing the beauty of spring and autumn (I.16). Here a parallellistic evocation

of the two seasons leads to a judgment that is entirely
aesthetic. Nukada first speaks of spring being so lush that
its glories cannot be fully appreciated:

> But, the hillsides being overgrown,
>   I may go among the foliage
>   yet cannot pick the flowers.
> The grass being rank,
>   I may pick
>   yet cannot examine them.

She then states a personal choice for the subtler and more
penetrable season, a choice which would be the standard
Japanese preference for the next thirteen centuries:

> Looking at the leaves
>   on the autumn hillsides,
> I pick the yellowed ones
>   and admire them,
> leaving the green ones
>   there with a sigh.
> That is my regret.
> But the autumn hills are for me.

"But the autumn hills are for me." *Akiyama ware wa*:
there is a tone of almost triumphant subjectivity here as
nature is penetrated by the poet's emotions, admiring, sigh-
ing, regretting.

As with other poems from this time, the structural effect
is one of symmetrical accretion, a style of imagination as-
sociated with the visual aesthetics of the age—couplets
aligned with a perfect simplicity like the three symmetrical
stories of the late seventh-century Yakushiji pagoda. Within
that structure, the land that in ritual verse had been an
affirmative reflection of the Emperor's power, an absolutely
symbolic entity beyond the whims of season or emotion,

has been raked by the poet's own sense of form into a landscape.

BY THE time that nature was yielding to Princess Nu-kada's aesthetic judgments, the poetry of Yamato had found its basic formal elements. Lacking both meter and rhyme, classical Japanese verse is based instead on a rhythm of phrases with alternating numbers of syllables. Already in the archaic songs included in the *Kojiki* and the *Nihon-shoki* we find patterns of long/short alternation—phrases of four syllables alternating with phrases of six, phrases of five syllables alternating with phrases of three, etc. By the middle of the seventh century this has largely settled into the five syllable/seven syllable rhythm which would rule Japanese poetic expression until modern times.

The two major forms in which the poets of *The Ten Thousand Leaves* composed are the *chōka* ("long poem") and the *tanka* ("short poem"). The *chōka* consists of a number of alternating five/seven phrases ending with a final seven/seven couplet:

5/7/5/7/5. . . .7/7

The number of five/seven phrases in a "long poem" ranges from a few to over a hundred (the *chōka* of Kaki-nomoto Hitomaro, especially, are examples of the form as sustained to a magnificent length). There are 260 *chōka* in *The Ten Thousand Leaves*.

The *tanka* consists of thirty-one syllables, arranged

5/7/5/7/7

It is easy to infer from this construction of the *tanka*, in five phrases identical to the final five of the *chōka*, that the shorter form is a crystallization of the *chōka* ending. Some recent Japanese scholarship suggests, however, that the *tanka* originated from an older form of verse called the *sedōka*, of which there are sixty examples in the anthology. The *sedōka* has a rhythm of

5/7/7/5/7/7

This repetition of two triplets is thought to be a characteristic of collective, popular song, making it easily chantable (often as a folk dialog). With the third phrase removed, however, it becomes

5/7/5/7/7

i.e., a *tanka*. In doing so, the form has lost its simple fluidity and gained instead a tension more suited to a sophisticated lyrical expression.

The Ten Thousand Leaves also includes a single example of the *bussokusekika*, the "Buddha's foot stone poem." There are twenty-one other examples of these poems on a stone located in the precincts of the Yakushiji temple. They are *tanka* to which an extra final phrase of seven syllables has been added (5/7/5/7/7/7), and generally not considered an independent form.

As the *chōka* waned in the eighth century, the *tanka* grew in importance. Approximately 4,200 of the 4,516 poems in *The Ten Thousand Leaves* are *tanka*. After *The Ten Thousand Leaves* the *chōka* disappeared as a viable form of poetry, and the *tanka* became the exclusive form until the rise of the *haiku* (with a 5/7/5 rhythm) in the seventeenth century.

Attached to most of the *chōka* in *The Ten Thousand Leaves* are satellite verses, in *tanka* form, called *hanka* or "envoys" (literally "repeating poems"). The envoy takes an imagistic or emotive theme from the *chōka*, often the lyrical statement which climaxes the longer poem, and brings it to a new expressive realization which in some cases is a fuller one than that in the *chōka* itself. This lyrical use of the *tanka* as envoy seems to be one reason for the development of the shorter form into its ultimate prominence as *the* vessel of the Japanese poetic impulse.

THE relationship between the *chōka* and its *tanka* envoys appears to be a key to understanding the work of Kakinomoto Hitomaro. Hitomaro is unquestionably the greatest poet of *The Ten Thousand Leaves* and, with Matsuo Bashō, who created the *haiku* as a form of art in the seventeenth century, one of the two most important figures in the history of Japanese poetry. Hitomaro's first recorded work is a *chōka* lament upon the sudden death of Crown Prince Kusakabe in 689, shortly before he was scheduled to assume the throne. Hitomaro's *chōka* (II.167) was composed for the Prince's "temporary enshrinement," during which various ceremonial tributes were intoned before the imperial bier prior to final burial. The poem moves, with an unprecedented scale and complexity, from a mythic panorama of the divine descent of the Emperors to an expression of earth's anticipation of the coming reign. These hopes are crushed by the Crown Prince's death, perceived as an unfathomable, even unreasonable, act of imperial will. The opening passage is an incremental cumulation of mythic images, echoing each other in a way that the twentieth-century *tanka* poet Saitō Mokichi called "symphonic":

> In the beginning
> of heaven and earth,
> on the riverbanks
> of the far firmament,
> the eight million deities,
> the ten million deities
> gathered in godly assembly
> and held divine counsel

These are Hitomaro's engines of heaven, and the *chōka* descends from them to terrestial metaphors, then to an expression of the public national grief, and finally to a blank lyrical statement of human bereavement:

> Now many days and months have passed
> since the voice of his morning commandments
> fell silent,
> and the Prince's courtiers
> do not know which way to turn.

The courtiers' grief and bewilderment is then given its own voice in two envoys:

> That the palace
> of the Prince I held in awe
> as I would look up
> to the far firmament
> should fall to ruins—
> alas!

> The crimson-gleaming sun
> still shines,
> but that the moon is hidden
> in the pitch-black night it crosses—
> alas!

> (II.168 and 169)

Both of these *tanka* present celestial images, symbolizing the mythic dimension of the Prince's death, which then lead to human cries of loss. They are repeating the poetic logic of the *chōka* itself in miniature, but with a heightened emotional intensity and directness. In Hitomaro's first appearance in *The Ten Thousand Leaves* he has opened up the *chōka*, and in his hands the form takes on a scale and elasticity it has never known before. And, by subjecting the *tanka* as envoy to the task of echoing the motive tension of the *chōka*, he is bringing the shorter poem to its own power as an independent, highly compacted lyrical form.

These two envoys are succeeded by twenty-four other *tanka* of bereavement. The first of these (II.170) is specifically attributed to Hitomaro, the others to the dead Prince's personal servingmen. But there can be little doubt that Hitomaro had a hand in the composition of the set. It is one of the earliest examples of a collective lyrical effort, a phenomenon which would be seen again in the banquet poetry of the eighth century. And it presages the development of the *renga* form in later centuries, in which *tanka* by several poets are integrated into a single collective composition.

Hitomaro is a poet without a biography. The only information we have about him comes from his poems and their headnotes in *The Ten Thousand Leaves* itself. We do know that the Kakinomoto clan was an old Yamato family, and one school of thought, represented by the late Orikuchi Shinobu, speculates that they were ceremonial reciters of ritual songs. Genealogical background may explain the only real "fact" we know about Hitomaro, his service to the Court (apparently with very low rank) as a composer of poems of praise and lament for the imperial family. It cannot, however, "explain" the conscious mind, with its own awareness of history, or the personal voice that begins to be heard from the suddenly expanded edifice of ritual language.

Hitomaro's first recorded step as a poet is a step backward, a rhetorical evocation of the mythic world, in whose eternal time the descent of the first Emperor from the "fields of heaven" is identical to the enthronement of the latest sovereign at the palace in Asuka. Hitomaro's task as a Court poet was one of crafting iconic images which "prove" the divinity of the imperial family. It was a task whose political basis may be traced back to two poems written following the victory of Emperor Tenji's younger brother in the succession dispute, known as the Jinshin War, which broke out after Tenji's death in 671. Upon defeating the forces of Tenji's son, this prince assumed the throne as Emperor Temmu in 673. Two *tanka* glorify Temmu's construction of his new palace in Asuka as a divine act. Here we find for the first time the words *kami ni shi maseba*, an explicit rhetorical device meaning "(because he is) a very god":

> Our Emperor,
> a very god,
> has turned the fields
> where red steeds wandered
> into his capital city.

> Our Lord,
> a very god,
> has turned the marshes
> where nested flocks of waterfowl
> into his imperial city.
>
> (XIX.4260 and 4261)

It is not the divinity of the Emperor which is new here, but the need to establish it explicitly in rhetorical language. This is a theme which Hitomaro would use in his iconic poetry. The simplest example is his turning a procession to Ikazuchi Hill by Empress Jitō, Temmu's widow and successor following the death of the Crown Prince, into a divine ascent, based on a conceit on the name "Ikazuchi," which means "thunder":

> Our Lord,
> a very god,
> builds her lodge
> above the thunder
> by the heavenly clouds.
>
> (II.235)

Many of Hitomaro's poems of praise are in the context of the imperial procession, a public, ritual event. They form the celebratory aspect of the same collective emotions of fealty which are expressed as cries of bereavement in the (equally public and ritual) laments for the imperial family.

The lament which Hitomaro composed upon the death of Prince Takechi in 696 (II. 199) is the longest *chōka* remaining. In its 149 phrases, all without a single Chinese word, is the battle scene which describes the Jinshin War. With the drumbeats that "boomed in our ears / like the very voice of thunder" and the arrows that "swarmed like a blinding swirl of snow," it is the single passage in Japanese poetry that comes closest to an "epic" style. It is not, however, an "epic" in the Western sense, for the extraordinary narrative power of the passage is folded into a larger scheme of collective lyricism. After the final procession to the Prince's tomb, the collective "we" of this lyric voice gaze back at the palace the Prince has left behind, vowing (did Hitomaro really believe it?) that it at least will last "ten thousand generations." The ending of the *chōka* and the envoys which follow express that typical situation of the bereaved courtiers—stunned and directionless as their ritual existence is robbed of its eternal justification. When the last procession breaks up, the courtiers who had lined up in their majestic, symmetrical ranks are left to wander lost in the present.

> Not knowing where they will drift,
> like the hidden puddles that run
> on the banks of Haniyasu Pond,
> the servingmen stand bewildered.

> (II.201)

The celebratory obverse of Hitomaro's masterpiece of public despair are the two *chōka*, each with an envoy (I.36-39), he composed at the time of a procession by Empress

Jitō to the detached palace on the banks of the Yoshino
River in the mountains south of Yamato. These are Hito-
maro's greatest achievements as provider of joyous icons
of imperial glory. Here the establishment of imperial di-
vinity assumes a specifically aesthetic dimension, achieved
through a parallelistic manipulation of the landscape. Ech-
oing Emperor Jomei's ritual assertion of Yamato's splendor
half a century earlier, the Empress, among all her lands,
"finds Yoshino good." But Hitomaro provides the aesthetic
reason: "for its crystal riverland among the mountains."
The Empress gazes down from her "blossom-strewn" dais
at the orchestrated movements of boats on patterned cur-
rents:

> And so the courtiers of the great palace,
> its ramparts thick with stone,
> line their boats
> to cross the morning river,
> race their boats
> across the evening river.
> Like this river
> never ending,
> like these mountains
> commanding ever greater heights,
> the palace by the surging rapids—
> though I gaze on it, I do not tire.
>
> (I.36)

This structuring of nature is like that in Princess Nu-
kada's experiments in symmetry, except that here the land-
scape is *peopled* with courtiers, those ever-present extras
in Hitomaro's ritual parades. Here the "proof" of the Em-
press' divinity is the very offering of this aesthetic order to
her, both figuratively by the courtiers in the poem and
literally by Hitomaro's presentation to her of a *chōka* which
artistically ratifies her political splendor.

In the lyrical envoy which follows (I.37), Hitomaro hopes

he can return to the scene of his ritual panorama as constantly as "the eternal moss / slick by the Yoshino River." Empress Jitō is actually recorded to have made thirty-one processions to Yoshino during her reign, and Hitomaro's expression of his own hope to return there seems to be overlapped with hers. Hitomaro is aware of what Yoshino has meant to this woman, who took refuge there during the Jinshin War with her husband Temmu and her son Kusakabe, both of them dead now. The *chōka*'s iconic portrayal of the Empress on her lofty dais seems to yield, in the *tanka*, to the hint of a *personality*, the shadow of a widow's mien.

This suggestion of character in a portrayal of an imperial figure is a development which becomes fully apparent in Hitomaro's poems (*chōka* and *tanka*) on a procession by Prince Karu, the dead Kusakabe's son, to the hunting fields of Aki. The *chōka* (I.45) begins with an iconic display of imperial power, as the eleven-year-old prince "manifests his divine will" and

> pushes through the mountains
> of Hatsuse, the hidden land,
> and bids yield to him
> the rough mountain road,
> lined with thick black pines,
> and the cliffs and the trees
> that block his path.

This objective glorification, at the same time suggestive of a personal reason for the Prince's determination, then gives way to an image of the boy searching for his father's soul, as the *chōka* ends with a lyrical portrayal of the child lost in the subjective act of memory:

> Grass for pillow,
> he sojourns the night,
> thinking of the past.

The *tanka* which "repeats" this situation turns the Prince even more into a character by detailing his motivation, by attributing to the semi-divine object of praise a psyche:

> The traveler sojourning
> on the fields of Aki
> stretches as in sleep,
> yet he cannot sleep,
> thinking of the past.   (I.46)

This is succeeded by three more *tanka*, in which the content of "the past," the symbolic mission of the procession—a reconnection with the dead Prince Kusakabe's soul—is made explicit. In the last of these *tanka*, the past is delivered to the present as images of the dead and the living are united in what Proust would have called their "common essence":

> The time—
> when the Crown Prince,
>   Peer of the Sun,
> lined his horses and set out
> on the imperial hunt—
> comes and faces me.   (I.49)

Within this remarkable conception of "time"—time given a spatial motion—the "common essence" linking the dead father and the living son, bringing them together "liberated from the contingencies of time," is none other than the position of each at the head of a hunting procession, the ritual stance itself.

The early history of Japanese poetry is a circle. Beginning with the naive ritual expression in an eternal time, it then develops a specifically aesthetic vision outside the bounds of ritual. With Hitomaro, it makes a conscious return to the ritual context. Finally, it uses that occasion for a daring imagistic transportation of the eternal realm of the imperial dead into commune with the present.

Hitomaro's exploitation of the ritual situation for lyrical purposes far more ambitious than Princess Nukada's is probably the most decisive act in the creation of Japanese poetry. Not only did he further develop the psychological portrayal of princes and princesses in their personal bereavement, but he also used "public" formulas and imagistic situations in his own "private" verse. Nakanishi Susumu, Japan's foremost living authority on *The Ten Thousand Leaves*, has pointed to the similarity between the description of Prince Karu as he "pushed through the mountains" in his symbolic quest for his dead father and Hitomaro's description of his own search on the mountain, in the stark and powerful ending of the first of two *chōka* "as he shed tears of blood following the death of his wife" (II.213):

> I struggled up here,
> kicking the rocks apart,
> but it did no good:
> my wife, whom I thought
> was of this world,
> is ash.

There is a high degree of imagistic and formulaic interplay within Hitomaro's poetry. It occurs not only between "public" and "private" expressions, but also between the three classical thematic categories of *The Ten Thousand Leaves*. These are "Poems on Various Themes" (*Zōka*), "Personal Exchanges" (*Sōmon*), and "Laments" (*Banka*, literally "coffin-pulling poems"). They largely consist, respectively, of the poetry of celebration, the poetry of longing, and the poetry of bereavement. Thus the "lament" often cited as Hitomaro's masterpiece, his *chōka* "upon seeing a dead man lying among the rocks on the island of

Samine in Sanuki" (II.220), begins with a panoramic ritual celebration of the land:

> Eternally flourishing,
>   with the heavens
>   and the earth,
>   with the sun
>   and the moon,
> the very face of a god—

Following this is a narrative description of the poet's journey through the Inland Sea to the island of Samine, where he discovers the corpse

> lying there
> on a jagged bed of stones,
> the beach
>   for your finely woven pillow,
> by the breakers' roar.

The *chōka* then climaxes with an image of longing for the lover who is on a journey—a typical situation in the "Personal Exchanges"—as Hitomaro ends his address to the dead man:

> If your wife knew,
> she would come and seek you out.
> But she does not even know the road,
>   straight as a jade spear.
> Does she not wait for you,
>   worrying and longing,
> your beloved wife?

Finally, having humanized the imperial demigods in his public *chōka*, Hitomaro manages now, in the second envoy succeeding this poem, to describe this lowly anonymous traveller with a sense of humanistic awe that almost suggests divinity:

> Making a finely woven pillow
> of the rocky shore
>   where waves from the offing
>   draw near,
> you, who sleep there!   (II.222)

Immediately following this exclamation of sympathy, heightened by Hitomaro's awareness of his own perilous journey, is another "journey poem," this time "by Kakinomoto Hitomaro in his own sorrow as he was about to die in the land of Iwami":

> Not knowing I am pillowed
> among the crags on Kamo Mountain,
> my wife must still be waiting
>   for my return.   (II.223)

This poem places Hitomaro in the same situation, with the same emotional overtones of longing and bereavement, as the dead man in his masterpiece. And it is followed by two poems in which his wife "responds," in "Personal Exchange" style, to his death poem. Her "responses" (which have him "strewn with the shells of Ishi River") are in turn followed by a poem in which another poet, "answering her with Hitomaro's supposed feelings," has Hitomaro "pillowed here beside the gems tossed ashore in the surging waves." Finally, this is followed by a variant similar to a poem Hitomaro wrote upon the death of an earlier wife!

It is clear from this spate of poetry, with all the different "explanations" of his death, that Hitomaro had already become a legend by the time his works passed into history (sometime after the first decade of the eighth century). His "biography" is already inextricable from the content of his poetry, as he becomes the object of his own lament and the world responds with elegiac repartee.

In ADDITION TO the sixteen *chōka* and sixty-three *tanka* (plus their variants) specifically recorded as being "written by Kakinomoto Hitomaro," *The Ten Thousand Leaves* also includes 330 *tanka*, thirty-five *sedōka*, and two *chōka* in what is known as "The Hitomaro Collection." A large number of these poems are not by Hitomaro. Other than a few poems which are obviously anachronistic, it is virtually impossible to distinguish which are by Hitomaro and which were merely attributed to him either because of a sensed similarity to his work or by a desire to associate a work with the glory of his already legendary name. Among "The Hitomaro Collection"—especially in Books Seven and Nine of *The Ten Thousand Leaves*—are found some of the finest achievements in the *tanka* form.

Hitomaro, as the creator of a full Japanese lyricism, is the hero of *The Ten Thousand Leaves*, and the central figure of its first three books, which represent the classical core of the anthology. Book One is a historical anthology of "Poems on Various Themes." Book Two, also arranged by historical periods, consists of "Personal Exchanges" and "Laments," while Book Three is a collection of all three categories (with the "Personal Exchanges" renamed "Metaphorical Poems").

Among the other poets represented in Book Three, Takechi Kurohito, a contemporary of Hitomaro, is important for his development of a personal voice in travel poetry. It is the lonely voice of the courtier who must journey away from the Court, who is forced to perceive nature outside its ceremonial contours.

Yamabe Akahito, who flourished in the generation of poets following Hitomaro's death, is also famous for his nature poetry. Many of his superbly crafted landscapes strive for the ritual pattern that Hitomaro attained in his "Yoshino" poems. But already by the first half of the eighth century the mythic intensity of Hitomaro's age is gone. In its place is an intricately realized objectivity (much admired by the early pioneers of modern Japanese poetry), images revealed within a motion which may be called "cinematic":

> Coming out
>   from Tago's nestled cove,
> I gaze:
>   white, pure white
> the snow has fallen
> on Fuji's lofty peak.   (III.318)

Book Four consists entirely of "Personal Exchanges," and Hitomaro is represented here as well, although not as prominently as in the first three books. The key word in the "Personal Exchanges" is *koi*. Often mistranslated as "love," its true meaning is "longing," a longing that, almost by definition, never attains its goal. The result is a diffuse, and invariably frustrated, eroticism that spreads over the world like a warm spring haze. Poem after poem speaks of gossip, of the prying eyes of men, of the inner intensity of passion concealed from others.

> This is a land of fearful gossip!
> Do not show your emotion,
>   do not be revealed in scarlet hues,
>   even if the longing kills you.   (IV.683)

The eroticism of *The Ten Thousand Leaves* is also highly formulaic. We will find an extremely passionate expression used in one poem for what seems to be a sexual repartee, and in another for a casual greeting between friends. But threading through all of the occasions of "personal exchange," whether specifically sexual or not, is a sense of the quality of longing itself. Its object is often a dreamlike, ambiguous image that appears to respond, but never with a definite yes or no.

Will I go on
merely hearing of you from afar—
    like the cranes that seem
    to cry in the dark night—
never meeting you?   (IV.592)

Both of these poems are from series of compositions by
a single poet, the first from "Seven poems by Lady Ōtomo
Sakanoue" (IV.683-689), the second from "Twenty-four
poems sent to Ōtomo Yakamochi by Lady Kasa" (IV.587-
610). The serialization of poetry in the "Personal Ex-
changes" suggests that, already by the eighth century, Jap-
anese poets are aware that the collection is artistically
greater than the sum of its individual *tanka*, a consciousness
of anthology itself as an organizing aesthetic principle. This
organizational impulse, whether applied to individual or
to collective composition, would be important for the com-
pilation of *The Ten Thousand Leaves* itself, and for the
imperial anthologies which form the landmarks of Japanese
poetry in the succeeding centuries.

This consciousness seems to be especially at work in the
compositions of Ōtomo Yakamochi, the young courtier to
whom so much of the longing in Book Four is addressed.
Yakamochi was the son of Ōtomo Tabito, and he grew up
under the influence of the poetry circle his father led at the
Dazaifu military headquarters in Kyushu (the works of
which are recorded in Book Five). Yakamochi is the most
prolific poet in *The Ten Thousand Leaves*, represented by
426 *tanka*, forty-six *chōka*, and one *sedōka*; most of his
poems are in Books Seventeen through Twenty. Yakamochi
is thought to have been one of the major compilers of *The
Ten Thousand Leaves*. Along with his own poetry, he is
important for having collected the "poems of the frontier
guardsmen" in Book Twenty.

In Yakamochi's "Personal Exchanges" in Book Four, we

can already see the "diaristic" quality that would characterize the great threads of self-consciousness, minute and exact, of his mature poetry in the last four books of the anthology. A strand of *tanka* from a series of fifteen he sent as part of an exchange with "the elder daughter of the Sakanoue house" (IV.741-755) suggests, along with a lyrical appeal to the girl, a journal of his own consciousness tortured with erotic yearning:

750

My desire had died,
I passed the time in quiet loneliness.
But then what compelled me to begin again
these half-hearted rendezvous
        that bring such pain?

751

Though several days
have yet to pass
since we saw each other,
how intensely I long for her,
driving madness upon madness!

752

What can I do
when she bears on my mind like this,
mere visions of her obsessing me?
What can I do
inside the thicket of men's eyes?

753

I thought that, after we had met,
my desire would be assuaged a while,
but now my longing rages all the more.

Along with the gathering of individual lyrical moments into strands of expression, another important development in the "Personal Exchanges" is that of the psychological metaphor. The oldest literary devices in Japanese are the epithetical formulas known (in terminology invented during the Heian Period) as "pillow words" (*makurakotoba*) and "preludes" (*joshi*). These were originally formulaically bound descriptions, used especially in introducing place names (*"heavenly* Kagu Hill," "Nara, *beautiful in blue earth*," etc.). They seem to have expressed a collective sense of the essential quality of a place. In the "Personal Exchanges" we see, emerging from this archaic form, a new, specifically metaphorical use of introductory expressions. One of the early examples occurs in an exchange between Emperor Tenji and Princess Kagami, in which the Princess writes:

> Like the hidden stream
> trickling beneath the trees
> down the autumn mountainside,
> so does my love increase
> more than yours, my Lord. (II.92)

Here nature provides an image of passion as an incremental force, an action of the emotions that, imperceptible at first, gathers in time. It is far more than a merely ornamental "prelude," for it brings off a dynamic interplay between nature and the psyche in a way similar to that of the Homeric simile. Again and again in *The Ten Thousand Leaves*, longing is the occasion for the birth of striking metaphorical images:

> Is it because my thoughts of her
> follow one upon another—
> like the bridge of planks

across the shallows of Mano Cove—
that I see my wife in my dreams?

(IV.490)

Is it for the rising of desire—
like the tide come spilling
up from the reedy shore—
that I cannot forget you?

(IV.617)

The astonishing ease with which the phenomena of nature are transformed into symbolic images of psychological states is one of the great accomplishments of Japanese literature. We can see its beginnings in the poetry of longing.

BOOK FIVE is unique in *The Ten Thousand Leaves*. First, it is a journal of the poetry circle which formed around Ōtomo Tabito at the Dazaifu military headquarters, and includes letters and essays as well as poems. And it is a record of Japanese poetry at a time when its composers were engaged in an enthusiastic acquisition of Chinese literary culture. The beginning of the eighth century saw the resumption of intercourse with the continent on a large scale. It was an age when the leader of a Japanese embassy to T'ang China, upon his return to Nara, appeared at Court to make his report in full Chinese dress. Book Five is full of letters written in Chinese in which one Japanese poet inquires of the other's well-being with allusions to Han Dynasty legends, or phrases his hope to meet the other soon with a gorgeous Chinese cliché such as "I await the time when a parting of the clouds may reveal to me your illustrious visage."

But, to the fortune of native literature, the poets of this age were not content merely to copy the Chinese, but applied their learning to compositions in their own language as well. Thus the above cliché is followed by a poem which weds the Chinese image of the "dragon steed" to the nostalgic desire of a Nara courtier to return to his capital, complete with its "pillow word."

> Would I could obtain
> a dragon steed right now,
> so I could fly
> to the capital at Nara,
> beautiful in blue earth. (V.806)

Ōtomo Tabito, the author of this *tanka* and the Chinese letter which precedes it, was the son of a chancellor and the scion of a once-great family that had begun its long decline. In the year 728, at the age of sixty-four, Tabito became Commander of the Dazaifu in Kyushu (at that time the island was known as Tsukushi). The Dazaifu had been established in the late seventh century as a "defense headquarters" near the Tsushima Straits, between Japan and Korea, at a time of expanding Chinese power in the Korean peninsula. By the eighth century the Dazaifu had become the imperial office overseeing the administration of southern Japan. Tabito remained there for three years until he was recalled to Nara and himself made Chancellor.

In 726 an official by the name of Yamanoue Okura, five years older than Tabito but of far lesser rank, had been appointed Governor of Chikuzen, a province within the Dazaifu jurisdiction. Okura is thought to have been by birth a Korean, whose family had emigrated to Japan during his childhood. He was a member of the embassy sent to China in 702, and seems to have spent at least two to three years studying on the continent. A poem by Okura appears among the "Thirty-two poems on the plum blossoms" (V.815-846) composed at a banquet held by Tabito at his Dazaifu residence in 730, and it is clear that Okura was the most talented member of Tabito's circle.

It is often said of these two enthusiasts of Chinese literature that Tabito was the Taoist, preferring the freedom of commune with nature, while Okura was the Confucianist, intent on his social and family responsibilities. The difference, however, does not seem to be a clear-cut philosophical one so much as a difference in personality. Book Three has a "Poem by Yamanoue Okura, upon leaving a banquet":

> Okura shall take his leave now.
> My child must be crying
> and its mother,
> who bears it on her back,
> must be waiting for me.   (III.337)

This is immediately followed by "Thirteen poems in praise of wine by Lord Ōtomo Tabito," among them what seems to be a response to Okura's self-righteous proclamation:

> Rather than making pronouncements
>   with an air of wisdom,
> it's better to down the wine
> and sob drunken tears.   (III.341)

There is definitely a dour side to Okura, most of whose remaining work was written while he was in his middle to late sixties. Tabito, though nearly as old, is never as obsessed with age and illness as is Okura. Tabito is comfortable in the "Personal Exchanges"; he is at his best in the world of the literary banquet, leading his guests in elegant conceits, exchanging cups of wine, and watching as "the plum blossoms opened like a spray of powder before a dressing mirror, and the orchids gave off a fragrance as from a purse of perfume." Only Okura could write a work like "An essay lamenting his own illness," a tour de force of disease and death, written in a Chinese that ranges over hundreds of lines from the heights of eloquence to the depths of pedantry and back again.

Yet it is his very seriousness, his rude withdrawal from Tabito's banquet of aestheticism, that, along with his profound apprenticeship in the Chinese and Buddhist classics, makes Okura the greatest poet between Hitomaro and Yakamochi. His "Poem sorrowing on the impermanence of life in this world" (V.804), his "Dialog of the Destitute" (V.892), his lament on the death of his son (V.904) are unique in Japanese poetry for their stark and relentless treatment of themes which are anything but elegant. In "An essay lamenting his own long illness" Okura speaks of a dead man being less than a living rat, then exclaims at the end of the essay, with the half-hearted remorse of a poet who has scandalized his audience, "How shameful of me to use a rat as an example!" Okura's work includes rats; it includes the empty rice pots of the poor; it does not shirk from describing the devastating effect of a fatal illness on his own child. Okura's is a humanistic lyricism that does not flow directly from what Hitomaro has created. Indeed, perhaps nothing testifies to the breadth of *The Ten Thousand Leaves* so much as the fact that it contains the work of both Hitomaro and Okura.

WHAT WE KNOW today as *The Ten Thousand Leaves* probably did not take its present form until sometime after 759, when Yakamochi wrote his last recorded poem. The initial process of compilation, in which Yakamochi participated, certainly went on into the last decades of the eighth century, and perhaps well beyond Yakamochi's death (ca.785) and into the ninth. The first half of the ninth century saw composition in Chinese rise to its greatest prestige, and interest in native verse suffered as a result. But *The Ten Thousand Leaves* is mentioned in the *Kokinshū* of 905, the first of the "imperial anthologies," which marks the reemergence of poetry in Japanese. In the preface to the *Kokinshū* its compiler, Ki no Tsurayuki, praises Hitomaro as the "saint of poetry" (*uta no hijiri*). But the first mention of *The Ten Thousand Leaves* "in twenty books" does not occur until 1086 (in the preface to the *Goshūishū* anthology). Clearly, we do not know what changes the poems and the original notes which follow them have undergone in the intervening centuries.

We do know that by the tenth century, with the invention of the native *hiragana* syllabary, *The Ten Thousand Leaves* had become unreadable. In 951 Emperor Murakami ordered a poet named Minamoto Shitagō to decipher its phonetic and semantic mix of Chinese characters. It was the beginning of a process that has occupied thousands of scholars through the centuries since. The most important of these scholars were the Priest Keichū in the seventeenth century and Kamo Mabuchi in the eighteenth. Their voluminous textual commentaries are the basis for the modern readings and interpretations of the anthology.

The process continues to this day. The most important work of twentieth-century scholarship, revolutionizing many of the old interpretations, has been Omodaka Hisataka's *Man'yōshū Chūshaku* ("*An Annotation of The Ten Thousand Leaves*") in twenty volumes (published by Chuōkōron Sha from 1957 to 1968). Among all the available modern texts, my reading of the anthology has benefitted most from Omodaka's work and from the new modern translation and commentary by Nakanishi Susumu, *Man'yōshū* (*The Ten Thousand Leaves*), the first volume of which appeared from Kōdansha in 1978.

Professor Nakanishi has been extremely generous with his time and advice, and kindly made available to me the galley proofs of his commentary before they were published. I am also grateful to Professor Earl Miner for his encouragement of this project and his reading of the manuscript, and to Miriam Brokaw of Princeton University Press for her continued interest and support. As a translator and a student of literature, I am indebted to John Nathan for years of inspiration.

This volume of the translation, incorporating Books One to Five, was begun while I was a dissertation fellow of the Japan Foundation. The Foundation has also provided support for the next volume (Books Six to Ten), and I wish to record my gratitude for its generous assistance.

Finally, I wish to express my thanks to Mrs. Tamura Kiyono of the Hiyoshi Kan in Nara, in whose venerable rooms much of this volume was first written, and to Ishibashi Sadao, my companion in the autumn of 1971 on the first of many trips to Nara and Asuka.

On an autumn night in the sprawling grounds of the Tōdaiji temple in Nara the only sound is the high-pitched cry of the deer, wandering among the monuments to which *The Ten Thousand Leaves* is so oblivious. The poets of Nara turned their attention to the deer's cry itself. They perceived longing in the eerie sound. *Uta*, the Japanese word for "song" or "poem," is originally *uttae*, an "appeal."

The cry stretches, and breaks, and then all that remain from the world of *The Ten Thousand Leaves* are its looming hills and silent fields.

Ian Hideo Levy

Ōtsuka, Tokyo
December, 1978

BOOK ONE

BY THE AUTHOR

The road alongside the mountains
(Yamanobe no michi)

POEMS ON VARIOUS THEMES

THE REIGN OF EMPEROR YŪRYAKU, WHO RULED THE REALM UNDER HEAVEN FROM THE ASAKURA PALACE IN HATSUSE (456-479)

1

Poem by the Emperor

Girl with your basket,
  with your pretty basket,
with your shovel,
  with your pretty shovel,
gathering shoots on the hillside here,
I want to ask your home.
Tell me your name!
This land of Yamato,
  seen by the gods on high—
it is all my realm,
in all of it I am supreme.
I will tell you
my home and my name.

THE REIGN OF EMPEROR JOMEI, WHO RULED
THE REALM UNDER HEAVEN FROM THE
OKAMOTO PALACE AT TAKECHI (629-642)

2

Poem by the Emperor when he climbed Kagu Hill
to view the land

Many are the mountains of Yamato,
but I climb heavenly Kagu Hill
    that is cloaked in foliage,
and stand on the summit
to view the land.
        On the plain of land,
smoke from the hearths rises, rises.
        On the plain of waters,
gulls rise one after another.
A splendid land
    is the dragonfly island,[1]
the land of Yamato.

3 and 4

Poem which Princess Nakatsu had Hashihito Oyu
present when the Emperor went hunting
on the fields of Uchi

Our Lord, sovereign
of the earth's eight corners,
in the morning

---

[1] "Dragonfly island" (*akitsushima*). The *Kojiki* "explains" this tradi-
tional epithet for Yamato with the incident, recorded during an excur-
sion to Yoshino by Emperor Yūryaku in which the Emperor was bitten
by a horsefly, which was in turn devoured by a dragonfly.

held and caressed
his catalpa bow.
In the evening
he stood beside it.
I can hear its golden tips resound.
Now he must be setting out
    on his morning hunt.
Now he must be setting out
    on his evening hunt.
I can hear the golden tips
of his catalpa bow resound.

Envoy

Lining his steeds
on the plain of Uchi,
he must be walking
over morning fields—
those fields so rank with grass!

5 and 6

*Poem written by Prince Ikusa as he looked at the
mountains where the Emperor had gone on his
procession to Aya County in the land of Sanuki*

Not even knowing
if the long spring day
has drawn through its mist
        into evening,
my heart,
    these twines of inner flesh,
            in pain,

weeping,
   like the tiger thrush,
        inside my soul—
like a strand of jewels,
it's fit to set this into words:

My Lord,
   that distant god,
passes through the mountains,
and the winds blow down
in the morning and the evening
to furl back my sleeves
here where I sojourn alone,
        grass for pillow.
Then even I
who thought I was a brave man
find my breast
   like the salt
      the fishergirls burn
        on Ami Cove,
afire with longing.

Envoy

Winds out of season
blow from the mountain pass,
and each night that I sleep
my heart is heavy with longing
for my wife back home.

    Considering the above poem with
    regard to the *Nihonshoki*, there are
    no processions to the land of Sanuki
    recorded in this reign. Also, the facts
    about Prince Ikusa are unclear.
    However, in Lord Yamanoue Okura's
    Forest of Classified Verse, it is

mentioned that the *Nihonshoki*
records a procession to the palace at
the hot springs of Iyo in winter, the
fourteenth day of the twelfth month,
of the eleventh year of the reign
(639).
In one book it is written that at this
time there were two trees in front of
the palace at Iyo. On these two trees
flocked two types of birds, the
hawfinch and the ladyfinch, in great
number. The Emperor ordered that
many ears of rice be hung on the
trees for them to eat. Then, the book
states, this poem was written.
Perhaps this procession continued
from Iyo to Sanuki.

THE REIGN OF EMPRESS KŌGYOKU, WHO RULED THE REALM UNDER HEAVEN FROM THE KAWAHARA PALACE IN ASUKA (642-644)

7

Poem by Princess Nukada

the events of which are yet unclear

I remember
our temporary shelter
by Uji's Palace ground,
when we cut the splendid grass
on the autumn fields
and sojourned under thatch.

Lord Yamanoue Okura's *Forest of
Classified Verse* states that one book
mentions this poem as having been
written in the fourth year of Taika
(648), at the time of the imperial
procession to the palace at Hira.

However, it is written in the
Nihonshoki that in spring, on the
third day of the fourth month, in the
fifth year of Empress Saimei's reign
(660), the Empress arrived at the hot
springs of Ki. In the third month the
Empress went on a procession to the
palace at Yoshino, and held a
banquet there. It is written that on
the third day of this month the
Empress proceeded to Hira Cove in
Ōmi.

THE REIGN OF EMPRESS SAIMEI, WHO RULED THE REALM UNDER HEAVEN FROM THE LATER OKAMOTO PALACE (655-661)

8

Poem by Princess Nukada

Wanting to board ship
in Nikita Harbor,
we have waited for the moon,
and now the tides too are right—
let us cast off!

Regarding the above poem, Lord
Yamanoue Okura's *Forest of
Classified Verse* comments with the
following considerations. On the
fourteenth day of the twelfth month
in the ninth year of Emperor Jomei's
reign (637),[2] the Emperor and
Empress made a procession to the hot
springs of Iyo. In spring, on the sixth
day of the first month, in the seventh
year of Empress Saimei's reign (661),

[2] This date is preceded by the four characters 元年己丑, "the first year of
the reign, *tsuchinotoushi*," which may either simply indicate the year in the
sixty-year cycle in which the reign began, or may mean that there was an
excursion this year (629) and *another one* in 637.

the imperial craft set into the sea
lanes for the west, to Kyushu. On the
fourteenth day the imperial craft
docked for the night by the
temporary palace of Iwayu by Nikita
Harbor. The Emperor went to view
things that had remained since past
ages, and was profoundly moved.
The commentary states that he then
expressed his sentiments by
composing this poem. Thus this is
considered to be a poem by the
Emperor. However, there are four
other poems on this occasion by
Princess Nukada.

9

*Poem written by Princess Nukada when she
went on a procession to the hot springs of Ki*

Gazing afar
over the stilled waves in the cove,
my husband stands there
beneath the divine oak.[3]

10-12

*Poems by Princess Nakatsu when she went to
the hot springs of Ki*

The span of your life,
    and of my life too,
is determined by the grass
    on Iwashiro Hill.
Come, let us bind it together.

[3] This is a translation based on the reading of the last two phrases of the
original as *shizumarishi / uranamimisake*, which is one of several possible
readings of the extremely controversial characters 莫囂圓隣之大相七兄
爪湯氣.

If you, my husband,
lack the grass to build
your temporary shelter,
cut the grass
   beneath the young pines.

You have shown me Nojima,
which I longed for,
but cannot pick me pearls
from bottom-deep Agone Bay.

> In Lord Yamanoue Okura's *Forest of
> Classified Verse*, this is considered to
> be a poem by the Empress.

13-15

Poem of the three hills by Nakatsu Ōe

> Later Emperor Tenji, who ruled the
> realm under heaven from the Ōmi
> Palace, 661-671

Kagu Hill
   loved Unebi's manliness,[4]
and Miminashi, with jealousy,
     rebuked her.
So it has been
since that age

---

[4] This follows Omodaka Hisataka's reading of the second phrase,
雲根火雄志等, as *Unebi wowoshi to* ("thought Unebi manly") rather than
the older reading of these characters as *Unebi wo woshi to*, which was thought
to mean "loved Unebi" or "found Unebi lovely". But "*woshi*" in *The Ten
Thousand Leaves* always means "to regret" rather than "to love." The newer
interpretation suggests two female hills fighting for the male hill Unebi,
rather than two male hills fighting for a female Unebi. For the full argument,
see Omodaka Hisataka, *Man'yōshū Chūshaku*, Vol. 1, pp. 138–139.

of the gods.
So it was
in ancient times,
and in our day too
mortals struggle for their mates.

Envoys

This plain of Inami,
where the god, rising,
came to watch
when Kagu Hill
and Miminashi fought.

This night,
when I have watched the sun
plunge through the long, furled
      banner of clouds
        into the sea,
let the moon shine clear!

THE REIGN OF EMPEROR TENJI, WHO RULED THE REALM UNDER HEAVEN FROM THE ŌTSU PALACE IN ŌMI (661-671)

16

When the Emperor ordered the Great Minister of the Center Fujiwara Kamatari to decide between the brilliance of the ten thousand blossoms on the spring hillsides and the colors of the thousand leaves on the autumn hillsides, Princess Nukada expressed her judgment with this poem.

When spring comes,
   bursting winter's bonds,
birds that were still
   come out crying
and flowers that lay unopening
   split into blossoms.
But, the hillsides being overgrown,
   I may go among the foliage
   yet cannot pick those flowers.
The grass being rank,
   I may pick
   yet cannot examine them.

Looking at the leaves of the trees
   on the autumn hillsides,
I pick the yellowed ones
   and admire them,
leaving the green ones
   there with a sigh.
That is my regret.
But the autumn hills are for me.

17-19

*Poem by Princess Nukada when she went down to the
land of Ōmi, with a poem by Princess Inoue
in response*

Though I would go looking back
   again and again
     upon Miwa Mountain,
       of the delicious wine,
until it recedes
     between the hills of Nara,
       beautiful in blue earth,
until the bends in this road
       heap high,
though I would long
   turn my distant gaze
     upon that mountain,
is it right that the clouds
should heartlessly conceal it?

Envoy

Thus do they hide Miwa Mountain?
Would that the clouds, at least,
     had sympathy,
for is it right
that they should conceal it?

     In Lord Yamanoue Okura's *Forest of
     Classified Verse*, the above two
     poems are stated to be imperial
     poems written upon looking back on
     Miwa Mountain when the capital
     was moved to the land of Ōmi. The

> *Nihonshoki* records that the capital
> was moved there in spring, on the
> nineteenth day of the third month, in
> the sixth year of Emperor Tenji's
> reign (667).

As the wild alders
on the rim of Hesogata's woods
shimmer in your clothes,
so you, my husband,
gleam in my eyes.

> The above poem, upon present
> consideration, does not seem to be a
> poem in response to Nukada's.
> However, in the old manuscript it
> was placed after it, so it has been left
> here.

20

*Poem by Princess Nukada when the Emperor went
hunting on the fields of Kamau*

Going this way on the crimson-
gleaming fields of *murasaki* grass,
going that way on the fields
of imperial domain—
won't the guardians of the fields
see you wave your sleeves at me?

21

Poem by the Crown Prince in response

> He was later Emperor Temmu, who
> ruled the realm under heaven from
> the Asuka Palace, 673-686.

If I despised you,
who are beautiful as the violet
from the *murasaki* grass,
would I long for you
though you are another's wife?

> In the *Nihonshoki* it is written that in
> summer, on the fifth day of the fifth
> month, in the seventh year of the
> reign (668), the Emperor went
> hunting on the fields of Kamau. At
> this time he was accompanied by the
> Crown Prince, the various Princes
> and Princesses, the Great Minister of
> the Center, and all the various
> ministers.

THE REIGN OF EMPEROR TEMMU, WHO RULED FROM THE KIYOMIHARA PALACE IN ASUKA (673-686)

22

During Princess To'ochi's pilgrimage to the shrine at Ise,
Fufuki Toji wrote this poem upon seeing the range of
crags at Hata

As moss does not grow
on cliffs soaring over the river,
so eternally may she
    remain a maiden.

It is yet unclear who Fufuki Toji was.
However, it is recorded in the
Nihonshoki that in spring, on the
thirteenth day of the second month,
in the fourth year of the reign (676),
Princess To'ochi and Princess Ae
made a pilgrimage to Ise.

23

*Poem written by someone in sorrow when Prince Omi
was exiled to Irago Island in the land of Ise*

Is Prince Omi,
   Omi of the beaten hemp,
a fisher, that he cuts
   the sleek seaweed
on Irago Island?

24

*Poem by Prince Omi, deeply moved upon hearing this
and replying*

Sorrowing for my life,
   life in this world,
drenched by the waves,
I cut sleek seaweed to eat
on Irago Island.

Considering the above poems with
reference to the *Nihonshoki*, it is
recorded that in summer, on the
eighteenth day of the fourth month,
in the fourth year of the reign (676),
Prince Omi, of the Third Rank, was
convicted of a crime and exiled to
Inaba. One of his children was exiled
to the Izu Islands, another to the
Chika Islands. However, his being

exiled here to the island of Irago in
the land of Ise may be a mistaken
notation by a later commentator
based on the words in the poem.

25

Poem by the Emperor

On Mimiga Peak
in beautiful Yoshino
snow was falling,
  unbounded by time,
rain was falling,
  without interval.
The road that I have come,
  deep in longing
  with every bend,
like the snow,
  unbounded by time,
like the rain,
  without interval -
O that mountain road!

26

A variant has,

On Mimiga Peak
in beautiful Yoshino
they say snow falls,
  outside the bounds of time,
they say rain falls,
  without interval.
The road that I have come,
  deep in longing
  with every bend,

like the snow,
   outside the bounds of time,
like the rain,
   without interval -
O that mountain road!

      Several phrases are not the same.
      Therefore both versions have been
      placed here.

27

*Poem by the Emperor, at the time of his
procession to Yoshino*

The good ones of the past
found Yoshino good,[5]
and often had a good look,
and spoke good of it.
Have a good look, my good one,
have a good look.

      In the *Nihonshoki* it is written that
      there was a procession to Yoshino on
      the fifth day of the fifth month in the
      eighth year of the reign (680).

---

[5] The poem is based on a pun on the name "Yoshino," which literally
means "good fields."

The Reign of Empress Jitō, Who Ruled the Realm Under Heaven from the Fujiwara Palace (686-697)

> In the eleventh year of her reign, she
> abdicated in favor of Crown Prince
> Karu and became the Retired
> Empress.

28

Poem by the Empress

Spring has passed,
and summer seems to have arrived:
garments of white cloth
hung to dry
on heavenly Kagu Hill.

29-31

*Poem written by Kakinomoto Hitomaro when he passed
the ruined capital at Ōmi*

Since the reign of the Master of the Sun
at Kashiwara by Unebi Mountain,
   where the maidens
     wear strands of jewels,
all gods who have been born
have ruled the realm under heaven,
each following each
like generations of the spruce,
     in Yamato
that spreads to the sky.

What was in his mind
that he would leave it

and cross beyond the hills of Nara,
  beautiful in blue earth?
Though a barbarous place
at the far reach of the heavens,
here in the land of Ōmi
where the waters race on stone,
at the Ōtsu Palace
in Sasanami
  by the rippling waves,
the Emperor, divine Prince,
ruled the realm under heaven.

Though I hear
this was the great palace,
though they tell me
here were the mighty halls,
now it is rank with spring grasses.
Mist rises, and the spring sun is dimmed.
Gazing on the ruins of the great palace,
its walls once thick with wood and stone,
I am filled with sorrow.

Envoys

Cape Kara in Shiga
at Sasanami
  by the rippling waves,
you are as before, but I
wait for courtiers' boats in vain.

Waters, you are quiet
in deep bends of Shiga's lake
at Sasanami
  by the rippling waves,

but never again may I
meet the men of ancient times.

32 and 33

*Poems written by Takechi Kurohito, sorrowing on the
ruined capital walls at Ōmi*

Am I one of the ancients
that, gazing on the ruined
capital at Sasanami
    by the rippling waves,
I am filled with sorrow?

The hearts of the gods
of the land of Sasanami
    by the rippling waves
have withered with grief,
and the capital lies in ruins.
Gazing, I am filled with sorrow.

34

*Poem by Prince Kawashima at the time of the procession
to the land of Ki*

> One book has Yamanoue Okura as
> the author.

How many generations
has the prayer cloth passed
hung from a branch
of the pine on the beach
where white waves break?

> In the *Nihonshoki* it is written that in
> autumn, the ninth month, of the

fourth year of Akamitori (690), the
Empress went on a procession to the
land of Ki.

35

Poem by Princess Ae when she crossed Se Mountain

Ah, here it is,
the one I loved back in Yamato:
the one they say lies by the road to Ki
bearing his name,
Se Mountain,
"mountain of my husband."

36-39

*Poems written by Kakinomoto Hitomaro at the time of
the imperial procession to the palace at Yoshino*

36

Many are the lands under heaven
and the sway of our Lord,
sovereign of the earth's eight corners,
but among them her heart
finds Yoshino good
for its crystal riverland
among the mountains,
and on the blossom-strewn
fields of Akitsu
she drives the firm pillars of her palace.

And so the courtiers of the great palace,
its ramparts thick with stone,
line their boats
to cross the morning river,

race their boats
across the evening river.
Like this river
never ending,
like these mountains
commanding ever greater heights,
the palace by the surging rapids—
though I gaze on it, I do not tire.

37

Envoy

Like the eternal moss
slick by the Yoshino River,
on which I do not tire to gaze,
may I never cease to return
and gaze on it again.

38

Our Lord
who rules in peace,
a very god,
manifests her divine will
and raises towering halls
above the Yoshino riverland
where waters surge,
and climbs to the top
to view the land.

On the mountains
folding upward around her
like a sheer hedge of green,
the mountain gods present their offerings.
They bring her blossoms in springtime

to decorate her hair
and, when autumn comes,
they garland her with scarlet leaves.
And the gods of the river
that runs alongside the mountains
make offerings for her imperial feast.
They send cormorants forth
over the upper shoals,
they cast dipper nets
across the lower shoals.
Mountain and river
draw together to serve her—
a god's reign indeed!

39

Envoy

A very god
whom mountain and river
draw together to serve,
she sets her boat to sail
over pools where waters surge.

> The *Nihonshoki* records imperial
> excursions to the palace at Yoshino
> in the first and eighth months of the
> third year of the reign (689), the
> second and fifth months of the fourth
> year (690), and the first and fourth
> months of the fifth year (691). It is
> unclear which occasion the poems
> were written upon.

40-42

Poems written by Kakinomoto Hitomaro when he stayed behind in the capital at the time of the imperial procession to Ise

On Ami Bay, the girls must now
be riding in their boats.
Does the tide rise
to touch the trains
of their beautiful robes?

On Cape Tafushi,
   hung with shell bracelets,
today also do the courtiers
cut the sleek seaweed?

Rowed by Irago Island
through the billows' roar:
does my lover ride that boat
round the rough island shore?

43

Poem by the wife of Tagima Maro

Where does my husband go?
Today is he crossing
Nabari Mountain
hidden in a deep
      inland place?

44

Poem by the Minister Isonokami Maro when he was accompanying the Empress

Is it for the height
  of Izami Mountain
(O let me see my wife)
that I cannot see Yamato,
or is it for the distance
      to my land?

Regarding the above poems, in the
Nihonshoki it is written that in
spring, on the third day of the third
month, in the sixth year of Akamitori
(692), Prince Hirose, of Jōkōshi
Rank, and others were left in
command of the palace while the
Empress was away. Then the
Chancellor, Miwa Takechimaro,
removed his cap rank and, presenting
it to the Court, spoke again and
again in remonstrance: "The imperial
carriage should not move just when
the farming period is about to
begin." On the sixth day the
Empress, refusing to heed his
remonstrance, finally set out on her
excursion to Ise.[6]

---

[6] The annotation goes on to say, "On the sixth day of the fifth month the Empress was at the temporary palace at Ago," but this refers to a different excursion, and apparently represents a misreading of the *Nihonshoki* on the annotator's part.

45

Poem written by Kakinomoto Hitomaro
when Crown Prince Karu sojourned on the
fields of Aki

Our Lord, sovereign
of the earth's eight corners,
child of the high-shining sun,
a very god,
manifests his divine will
and leaves behind
the firmly-pillared capital.

He pushes through the mountains
of Hatsuse, the hidden land,
and bids yield to him
the rough mountain road,
lined with thick black pines,
and the cliffs and the trees
that block his path.

In the morning, like a bird,
he crosses the hills.
As evening falls
faint as jewel's light,
he pushes aside
the pampas grass
that waves in banners
and the dwarf bamboo
on the broad
and snow-fallen
fields of Aki.
Grass for pillow,
he sojourns the night,
thinking of the past.

46-49

Tanka

The traveler sojourning
on the fields of Aki
stretches as in sleep,
yet he cannot sleep,
thinking of the past.

A wild field
where they cut the splendid grass,
but we have come to remember our Lord,
gone like the yellowed leaves of autumn.

On the eastern fields
I can see the flames of morning rise.
Turning around,
I see the moon sink in the west.

The time—
when the Crown Prince,[7]
   Peer of the Sun,
lined his horses and set out
on the imperial hunt —
comes and faces me.

50

Poem by the builders of the Fujiwara Palace

Our Lord, sovereign
of the earth's eight corners,
child of the high-shining sun,

[7] Crown Prince Kusakabe. See poem no. 167.

a very god,
has determined to rule her lands
at a site by Fujiwara,
   of the rough wisteria cloth,
there to raise aloft her palace halls.
As even heaven and earth
have drawn together to serve her wish,
so men took timber of cypress,
      split thick pines,
from Tanakami Mountain
in the land of Ōmi,
where the waters race on stone,
and floated it,
   like sleek seaweed,
down the Uji River,
   of the eighty warrior clans.
The Empress' people,
rushing to gather it,
forgetting their homes,
with no care for themselves,
plunged in and bobbled
   like so many ducks.
They hauled the thick pine timber
to the Izumi River
where, from the Kose Road
(the path which draws in
lands yet disobedient
to the heavenly palace we build),
there appeared a miraculous turtle,
and on its back the inscription:
"Our land shall be forever."
They have turned the timber into rafts,
            near a hundred,

and are floating them upstream.
As we watch how they strive,
our Lord indeed
    seems a very god.

> In the *Nihonshoki* it is written that in
> autumn, the eighth month, of the
> seventh year of Akamitori (693), the
> Empress went on a procession to the
> site of the Fujiwara Palace. In spring,
> the first month, of the eighth year
> (694), she went on a procession to
> the new palace. In winter, on the
> sixth day of the twelfth month, the
> reign was transferred to the Fujiwara
> Palace.

51

*Poem by Prince Shiki after the move from the Asuka
Palace to the Fujiwara Palace*

Asuka winds
furling back courtmaidens' sleeves:
the capital is far away,
and they blow in vain.

52

Poem of the Imperial Well at the Fujiwara Palace

Our Lord, sovereign
of the earth's eight corners,
child of the high-shining sun,
founds her great palace
on the fields of Fujii,
    of the rough wisteria cloth,

BY THE AUTHOR

The present-day village of Asuka

Asuka winds
furling back courtmaidens' sleeves:
the capital is far away,
and they blow in vain.

> Prince Shiki ("after the move from the Asuka Palace to the
> Fujiwara Palace," I.51)

and stands there on the banks
of Haniyasu Pond.

Around her she sees
Yamato's green Kagu Hill
standing lush
towards the Eastern Gate,
    a hill of spring,
and this hill, Unebi,
rising newly verdant
towards the Western Gate,
    young and fresh,
and Miminashi,
that hill of green sedge,
standing towards the Northern Gate,
    superb, like a very god,
and Yoshino Mountain—
beautiful its name—
soaring beyond the Southern Gate
    in the distance, among the clouds.

Here in the divine shadows
of high-ruling heaven,
in the divine shadows
of heaven-ruling sun,
may these waters gush forever,
the crystal waters
        of her imperial well.

53

Tanka

Maidens born
into a line that serves
the great palace at Fujiwara—
how I envy them!

> The name of the author of the above
> poems is yet unknown.

54-56

Poems written in autumn, the ninth month, of the first
year of Taihō (701), when the Retired Empress went on
a procession to the land of Ki

54

While my trailing, trailing eyes
   watch camellias
trailing, trailing in a row
   on Kose Mountain,
my mind would contemplate
the Kose fields in spring.

> The above poem is by Sakato
> Hitotari.

55

How I envy the people of Ki—
land good in hempen cloth—
who can see Matsuchi Mountain
while they come and while they return.
How I envy the people of Ki!

> The above poem is by Tsukino'obito
> Ōmi.

56

A variant has (for 54),

My trailing, trailing eyes
do not tire to gaze on camellias
trailing, trailing in a row
by the riverside,
on those Kose fields in spring.

> The above poem is by Kasuga Oyu.

Poems at the time of the Retired Empress'
procession to the land of Mikawa in the
second year (702)

57

Go into the field,
and run among the black alders
fragrant on the Hikuma Plain.
Catch the scent in your clothes
as a souvenir of your journey.

> The above poem is by Naga
> Okimaro.

58

Where does it go for harbor,
　　the tiny boat,
　　　　with no gunwales,
that they rowed around Cape Are?

> The above poem is by Takechi
> Kurohito.

59

Poem by Princess Yoza

In the cold night,
when winds blow upon your wife,
whose life flows away without you,
do you, my husband, sleep alone?

60

Poem by Prince Naga

Is it at Nabari,
　　hidden like the morning face
　　　　after the evening tryst,
that my woman has taken lodge so long?

61

Poem written by the Toneri maiden while accompanying the imperial procession

Round like the targets brave men face
and, squeezing in their fingers
beast-subduing arrows, shoot,
Matokata is clear and refreshing to my eyes.[8]

62

Poem by Kasuga Oyu when Mino Okamaro crossed to enter China

In the Tsushima crossing,
    where the island peak stands splendid,
tie a prayer cloth over the ocean depths
and quickly return!

63

Poem by Yamanoue Okura when he was in China thinking of his native land

Come lads, make speed
for Yamato! The pines
on the beach
by Ōtomo's noble cove
wait for us in longing.

[8] This poem is based on a pun on the name "Matokata," the first two syllables of which mean "target" (的 *mato*).

64 and 65

Poems at the time of the procession
to the palace at Naniwa in the third year
of Keiun (706)

Poem by Prince Shiki

On the cold evening, when frost
glazes the pinioned wings of ducks
as they swim by the reedy shore,
it is of Yamato I think.

Poem by Prince Naga

O I do not tire
to gaze, with the maiden
        Otohi,
on Suminoe, on Matsubara,
the sparse field of pines
        struck by hail.

Poems at the time of the Retired Empress' procession to
the Palace at Naniwa

66

Accompanying my Lord to Ōtomo,
I make my pillow
    on the roots of a pine
        on Takashi Beach,
and sleep, yet still
I think of my home.

    The above poem is by Okisome
    Azumahito.

67

Journeying, I fall into longing
                over things,
yet if I could not hear
            the crane's voice,
I would die of longing.

> The above poem is by Takayasu
> Ōshima.

68

Halfshell on the beach
by Ōtomo's noble cove,
shell of forgetfulness:
but could I ever forget
my wife back home?[9]

> The above poem is by Prince
> Mutobe.

69

If I had known
    you, my Lord, were journeying,
            with grass for pillow,
I would have dyed your clothes
with red clay from the cliffs.

> The above poem was presented by
> the maiden of Suminoe to Prince
> Naga. Her surname and personal
> name are yet unclear.

[9] The "shell of forgetfulness" (*wasuregai*) apparently is based on the popular belief that finding a halfshell on a beach made one able to forget the lover one was longing for.

70

*Poem by Takechi Kurohito when the
Retired Empress went on a procession to the
palace at Yoshino*

Has the calling bird
come crying to Yamato?
Its call soars
across Kisa's mountain recesses
and passes toward the capital.

71 and 72

*Poems at the time of the late Emperor Mommu's
procession to the palace at Naniwa*

Longing for Yamato,
I cannot sleep my sleep.
Then is it right that cranes
should heartlessly cry
here where the beach
juts into the sea?

> The above poem is by Osakabe
> Otomaro.

I shall not row to the offing
where they cut the sleek seaweed.
I cannot forget the one
who lay beside
my well-woven pillow.

> The above poem is by the Minister of
> Ceremonies Fujiwara Umakai.

73

Poem by Prince Naga

Winds on the
beach—quick
as I would go to see my wife—
blow without fail
    upon that camellia
waiting for me in Yamato.

74 and 75

Poems at the time of the late Emperor Mommu's
procession to the palace at Yoshino

Though chill is the storm
on beautiful Yoshino Mountain,
perhaps yet this night too
I may be sleeping alone.

    One source says that the above is a
    poem by the Emperor.

Chill are the morning winds
on Ujima Mountain,
but my wife is not here
to give me clothes for my journey.

    The above poem is by Prince Naga.

The first year of Wadō (708)

76

Poem by the Empress

I can hear the bowstrings twang
on the brave men's leather armbands
as the warriors' general
stands the shields for drill.

77

Poem presented by Princess Minabe in response

Do not worry over things, my Lord,
for I am ever by your side,
where the gods have bestowed me.

78

*In spring, the second month, of the third year of
Wadō (710), the capital was moved from the Fujiwara
Palace to the Nara Palace. The following poem was
written at this time, as the imperial carriage was stopped
on the fields of Nagaya and the poet gazed back in the
distance at our old home.*

> In one book it is written that this is a
> poem by the Retired Empress.

If I depart, and leave behind
the village of Asuka,
    where the birds fly,
I shall no longer be able
to see the place where you abide.

79

*One book has the following poem, on the
occasion of the move from the
Fujiwara Palace to the Nara Palace*

In awe of our Emperor's command,
we left our homes,
    and our soft living,
and set our ships afloat
down Hatsuse River,
   down that hidden land.
Not one of its eighty bends
did we sail by
without looking back
ten thousand times.

We trod til dusk
came over our path,
   straight as a spear of jade,
and reached the Saho River
by the capital at Nara,
   beautiful in blue earth.
As we perceived the morning moon
crystalline above our sleeping clothes
we saw, where evening frost had fallen
white as brilliant mulberry cloth,
the river frozen
like a bed of stone.

Come, o Lord, into the house
that we have toiled,
    back and forth,
in that chill night,
      unresting,

to build you. Come
for a thousand generations
and I too shall go
    back and forth
there, to serve you.

80

Envoy

I too shall go back and forth
to your house in Nara,
   beautiful in blue earth,
for ten thousand generations.
Do not think I may forget.

> The name of the author of the above
> poems is yet unknown.

81-83

*Poems written by the imperial well at Yamanohe when
Princess Nagata was sent to the Shrine of our offerings
at Ise, in summer, the fourth month, of the fifth year of
Wadō (712)*

There,
as I saw the imperial well
at Yamanohe,
I met the maidens of Ise,
   Ise of the divine wind.

My heart is full
with withering sadness
as I watch the showers
stream from the far heavens.

When will I cross Tatsuta Mountain
  (like the white waves rising
  on the far fathomless offing)?
I would see the place
where my wife dwells.

> The last two poems, on present
> consideration, bear no resemblance to
> the poem on the imperial well.
> However, perhaps they were ancient
> poems recited on the occasion.

THE ERA OF THE NARA PALACE (710-784)

84

*Poem written when Prince Naga banqueted with Prince
Shiki at the Palace at Saki*

If autumn were here
these would be mountains
as we see them now,
where the deer cries
in longing for his wife—
on these high fields.[10]

> The above poem is by Prince Naga.

---

[10] Apparently they are looking at a painting of a deer.

BOOK TWO

BY THE AUTHOR

The sepulchral mound in Asuka where Emperor Temmu and
Empress Jitō lie buried together

Our Lord,
who, while we trembled,
fixed the far and heavenly
halls of his shrine
on the fields of Makami in Asuka
and, godlike, has secluded himself
in the rocks there. . . .

Kakinomoto Hitomaro (from "Poem at the time of the
temporary enshrinement of Prince Takechi at Kinoe,"
II.199)

PERSONAL EXCHANGES

THE REIGN OF EMPEROR NINTOKU, WHO RULED
THE REALM UNDER HEAVEN FROM THE TAKATSU
PALACE IN NANIWA (313-398)

85-88

Four poems by Empress Iwanohime, thinking of the
Emperor

You journey, and the days
have turned long.
Shall I go search into the mountains,
  there to greet you,
or shall I wait and wait?

  The above poem is in Yamanoue
  Okura's *Forest of Classified Verse.*

Instead of longing for you
  like this,
would that I could die,
pillowed in the crags
of a towering mountain.

I shall wait for you
  like this
as long as I live,
until the frost
cakes my trailing black hair.

Morning mists hover
upon the rice ears
in the autumn fields.
Which way
will my longing disappear?

89

A variant has,

Til dawn unsleeping
I shall wait for you,
though my pitch-black hair
be covered with the dew.

> The above poem is in *An Anthology
> of Ancient Poems.*

90

In the Kojiki *it is written that Crown Prince Karu
committed incest with his maternal sister, Princess Karu
no Ōiratsume, and was therefore banished to the hot
springs of Iyo. At this time she, Princess Sotohori,
unable to bear her longing, followed him, and composed
this poem.*

You journey, and the days
have turned long.
I shall go to greet you,
like the elder-tree on the mountain.
I cannot wait and wait.

> The *Kojiki* and the *Forest of Classified Verse*
> have differing explanations of the above poem.
> They also differ as to authorship. Referring
> then to the *Nihonshoki,* we find it states that
> in spring, the first month, of the twenty-second

year of Emperor Nintoku's reign (333), the
Emperor told the Empress of his intention to
wed Princess Yata and install her as a consort.
The Empress would not hear of it. The
Emperor wrote her a poem begging her to
consider it. In autumn, on the eleventh day of
the ninth month, in the thirtieth year of the
reign (342), the Empress went on a procession
to the land of Ki. Arriving at Cape Kumano,
she picked leaves of the *mitsuna* oak to take
back to the capital. At this time the Emperor,
hearing that the Empress was away, took
Princess Yata as a bride and wed her in the
palace. When the Empress arrived at the
Naniwa ford, she heard that the Emperor had
been with Princess Yata, and was greatly
resentful, and so on.

Another passage in the *Nihonshoki* states that
in spring, on the seventh day of the first
month, in the twenty-third year of Emperor
Ingyō's reign (434), Prince Kinashi no Karu
was made Crown Prince. His features were
handsome, and those who looked on him
found themselves in love with him. His
maternal sister, Princess Karu no Ōiratsume,
also had fine features, and so on. They ended
up having secret intercourse, somewhat
relieving their unbearable desire. In summer,
the sixth month, of the twenty-fourth year of
the reign (436), the Emperor's soup froze and
turned to ice. Astonished, the Emperor had the
cause divined. The diviner stated that there
was a disturbance within the palace. He
suspected incest. Therefore the Emperor had
Princess Ōiratsume banished to Iyo.

The above poem appears in neither of these
two reigns nor these two incidents.

THE REIGN OF EMPEROR TENJI, WHO RULED THE REALM UNDER HEAVEN FROM THE ŌTSU PALACE IN ŌMI (662-671)

91

Poem given by the Emperor to Princess Kagami

Constantly I would gaze
upon your house.
Would that my house
were on Ōshima Peak
      in Yamato.

92

Poem by Princess Kagami in response

Like the hidden stream
trickling beneath the trees
down the autumn mountainside,
so does my love increase
more than yours, my Lord.

93

*When Lord Fujiwara, Great Minister of
the Center, asked Princess Kaga to wed him,
she sent him this poem*

The jewelled box is easily opened,
and the night, opening into dawn,
saw you leave. What of your name
if this be known?
      My regrets are for my own.

94

Poem by Lord Fujiwara, Great Minister of the Center,
answering Princess Kagami

Crawling vines
    on Mimoro Mountain
        of the jewelled box:
I shall not be able to bear
not sleeping with you.

95

Poem by Lord Fujiwara, Great Minister of
the Center, composed when he wed the
courtmaiden Yasumiko

Hey, I've got Yasumiko!
    the one they all said
        was impossible to get—
I've got Yasumiko!

96-100

Five poems when Priest Kume asked Lady Ishikawa to
wed him

The Priest:

If I pull the string
of the true bow
    from Shinano,
        where they cut fine reeds,
I fear that you will play the snob
and say, "No, don't!"

The Lady:

I say I do not know
a way to fit the string
without bending the true bow
   from Shinano,   ·
      where they cut fine reeds.

The lady:

If you bend the catalpa bow
I will sway to your will,
and yet I fear I cannot know
how afterwards your heart will go.

The Priest:

The one who fits the string
to his catalpa bow
and bends it back to shoot—
he is the one who knows
the line his heart shall follow.

The Priest:

Like the cords that bind to horses
boxes filled with first ears of rice
that Eastern people bring for tribute,
it seems my girl
      is harnassed to my heart.

101

Poem by Ōtomo when he asked Lady Kose to wed him

> His personal name was Yasumaro.
> He was the sixth son of Lord Ōtomo
> Nagatoko, Minister of the Right at
> the Naniwa Court. During his life
> Yasumaro served as Chancellor and
> Commanding General at the Nara
> Court.

They say a raging god
clings to the tree that bears no fruit,
to every tree,
    like the jewelled vine,
        that bears no fruit.

102

Poem by Lady Kose in response

> She was Lord Kose Hito's daughter.
> He was Chancellor at the Ōmi Court.

Whose love is it
that, like the jewelled vine,
flowers but bears no fruit?
It is I who think of you with longing.

THE REIGN OF EMPEROR TEMMU, WHO RULED THE REALM UNDER HEAVEN FROM THE KIYOMIHARA PALACE IN ASUKA (673-686)

103

*Poem sent by the Emperor to his concubine
of the Fujiwara family*

A great snow has fallen
on my village.
Only later will it fall
on that antiquated village,
       your Ōhara.

104

*Poem presented by his concubine of the
Fujiwara family in response*

I have spoken
to the god of waters on my hill,
urging him to make it snow.
Those flakes must now
be falling where you are.

THE REIGN OF EMPRESS JITŌ, WHO RULED THE REALM UNDER HEAVEN FROM THE FUJIWARA PALACE (686-697)

105 and 106

Two poems by Princess Ōku when her brother
Prince Ōtsu left to return to the capital
after a secret visit to the Shrine at Ise

Letting my man
    away to Yamato,
I stand here as the night deepens,
drenched with dew before twilight.

The autumn mountains
are hard to pass through
even when two go together.
How, my Lord, will you
cross over them alone?

107

Poem sent by Prince Ōtsu to Lady Ishikawa

Waiting for my girl
in the trickling rain
on the foothill-trailing mountain,
I stand here drenched
in that trickling mountain rain.

108

Poem presented by Lady Ishikawa in response

You say you have been drenched
waiting for me
on the foothill-trailing mountain.
O that I could be
that trickling rain!

109

*Poem by Prince Ōtsu when Tsumori Tōru discovered
through divination that the Prince had secretly wed Lady
Ishikawa*

Knowing full well
it would be told
in Tsumori's divination
(Tsumori of the great boat),
we two did sleep together.

110

Poem sent by the Crown Prince, Peer of the Sun,[1] *to
Lady Ishikawa*

 The Lady's name was Ōnako.

How could I ever forget Ōnako?
Not for as little
as a palmful of the grass
they cut on distant fields.

---

[1] Crown Prince Kusakabe. See poem no. 167.

111

Poem sent by Prince Yuge to Princess Nukada during the
imperial procession to Yoshino

Is it a bird
longing for the past
that soars crying
over the imperial well,
there by the evergreen?

112

Poem presented by Princess Nukada in response

The bird you say
longs for the past
is the cuckoo.
Its cry must echo what I feel.

113

When he sent Princess Nukada a moss-covered pine
branch from Yoshino, she sent him this poem

Ah, I love the branch
from the jewel-like pine
in splendid Yoshino,
for it comes with word from you.

114

Poem by Princess Tajima when she was staying at Prince Takechi's palace thinking of Prince Hozumi

As the ears of rice
on the autumn fields
bend in one direction,
so with one mind would I bend to you,
painful though the gossip be.

115

Poem by Princess Tajima when Prince Hozumi was ordered by imperial command to the mountain temple at Shiga

Rather than being left behind
and longing,
I would go catch up with you.
Tie your signs
to the bends of the road, my man!

116

Poem by Princess Tajima after she had secretly met Prince Hozumi while staying at Prince Takechi's palace, and the fact had gotten out

Because men's talk clusters,
because the gossip is painful,
I cross the morning river
that never in my life
have I crossed before.

117

Poem by Prince Toneri

"Does a brave man fall
in unrequited love?"
I grieve, and yet
this fool of a brave man
has fallen into longing.

118

Poem by Princess Toneri, responding

It is because
a brave man grieves
in his longing for me
that my hair is drenched
    and come undone.

119-122

Four poems by Prince Yuge, thinking of
Princess Ki

Quick stream the rapids
in the Yoshino River.
Never stagnant for an instant,
I would have our love go on.

Rather than keep longing
    for my girl,
I would be a flower
of the autumn bush clover,
bloomed and fallen.

Evening comes, and the tides
rise into Asaka Cove in Suminoe.
I want to be cutting
        the sleek seaweed there.

Swaying like the harbor waters
where a great ship has berthed,
I have become thin with worry—
though she is another's girl.

123-125

*Three poems composed when Mikata Sami took to
his bed with sickness shortly after wedding the daughter
of Sono Ikuha*

Mikata Sami:

Raised up, it falls back down.
Unraised, it lies too long.
Lately I cannot see my girl's hair.
Can it be she's raised it up?

The Maiden:

They all say my hair
is now too long
and tell me, "Raise it up,"
but what matter if this hair you saw
should lie dissheveled?

Mikata Sami:

The road I tread
in the shadow of the orange trees
forks eight ways
and things confuse me,
unable to meet my girl.

126

Poem sent by Lady Ishikawa to Ōtomo Tanushi

> He was the second son of the Saho
> Chancellor, Lord Ōtomo Yasumaro.
> His mother was Lady Kose.

I heard you were
      a courtly knight,
but you refused me shelter
and sent me away.
Dull courtier are you!

> Ōtomo Tanushi's personal name was Chūrō.
> He cut a dazzling figure, the epitome of
> courtly style. None who looked on him or
> heard of him could keep from sighing. At this
> time there was one called Lady Ishikawa.
> Wanting to wed him, she constantly bemoaned
> her solitude. In her heart she desired to
> approach him with a letter, but she had yet to
> find an appropriate messenger. Thereupon she
> came up with a plan whereby she went to his
> house herself, made up as a poor old woman.
> Dangling a clay pot, she reached the side of
> his sleeping quarters. Tottering toward his
> door, she knocked and said in a choking old
> voice, "It's the poor woman who lives east of
> your house, come to get some kindling fire."
> She was hidden in the dark, and Chūrō could
> not see through her disguise. To her own
> surprise, she found she could not bring herself

to go ahead with her plan to seduce him.
Letting things go at that, she took the kindling
fire and set back on the road she had come. In
the morning she was both embarrassed that
she, a woman, had approached him on her
own, and regretful that her heart's
expectations had gone unfulfilled. Therefore
she composed this poem and sent him the
teasing verse.

127

Poem sent by Ōtomo Tanushi in response

I am the courtly knight.
It is I,
   who refused you shelter
and sent you away,
who am the courtly knight.

128

*Another poem sent by this same Lady Ishikawa to
Ōtomo Tanushi Chūrō*

Just as in the rumors
   I have heard,
my man who totters
on feet frail as reed buds,
take care!

> She sent the above poem inquiring of
> Chūrō when he was sick with an
> illness of the feet.

129

Poem sent by Lady Ishikawa, a lady-in-waiting at the
palace of Prince Ōtsu, to Ōtomo Sukunamaro

> Her personal name was Lady
> Yamada. Sukunamaro was the third
> son of Lord Ōtomo, the Chancellor
> and Commanding General.

Wizened hag am I
to sink like this
into such longing,
like a very child!

130

Poem given by Prince Naga to the Prince, his brother

You do not cross
the rapids of the Niu,
and your heart races
with a painful longing.
Come over, my brother, to me!

131-137

*Two poems by Kakinomoto Hitomaro when he parted
from his wife in the land of Iwami and came up to the
capital*

with tanka

131

I.

People may say that Tsuno Cove
in the land of Iwami
has no good inlets,
they may say it has no good lagoons,
but I don't care.
Though it has no good inlets,
I don't care.
Though it has no good lagoons,
the wind, with morning wings,
and the waves, with evening wings,
carry over those whale-hunted seas
to the desolate beach in Nikita harbor
green, sleek seaweed,
seaweed from the offing,
and the memory of my wife,
whom I left there
    as mist and frost
        are left on the ground,
who swayed to my side in sleep
    like sleek seaweed
swaying to and fro with the waves.

Though I look back ten thousand times
from each of this road's eighty bends,

my village has receded
farther and farther in the distance.
Higher and higher
are the mountains I have crossed.
That I might gaze on my wife's door
where she in her longing
wilts like the summer grass,
mountains, bend down!

132 and 133

Envoys

O does my wife
see the sleeves I wave
from between the trees
on Takatsuno Mountain in Iwami?

The whole mountain is a storm
of rustling leaves
of dwarf bamboo,
but I think of my wife,
having parted from her.

134

One version has for one of the envoys,

I wonder if my wife
saw me waving my sleeves
from between the trees
on Takatsuno Mountain in Iwami.

135

II.

At Cape Kara[2]
on the Sea of Iwami,
where the vines
   crawl on the rocks,
rockweed of the deep
grows on the reefs
and sleek seaweed
grows on the desolate shore.
As deeply do I
think of my wife
who swayed toward me in sleep
   like the lithe seaweed.
Yet few were the nights
we had slept together
before we were parted
like crawling vines uncurled.
And so I look back,
still thinking of her
with painful heart,
this clench of inner flesh,
but in the storm
of fallen scarlet leaves
on Mount Watari,
crossed as on
      a great ship,
I cannot make out the sleeves
she waves in farewell.

---

[2] Preceding "Cape Kara" is an untranslatable epithet, "*koto saeku.*" "Kara" also means "China," and the epithet's meaning, "babbling words," refers to the incomprehensible foreign tongue. This is a purely formal pillow-word— a pun—and has nothing to do with the place Cape Kara itself.

For she, alas,
is slowly hidden
like the moon
   in its crossing
      between the clouds
over Yagami Mountain
just as the evening sun
coursing through the heavens
has begun to glow,
      and even I
who thought I was a brave man
find the sleeves
of my well-woven robe
drenched with tears.

136 and 137

Envoys

The quick gallop
of my dapple-blue steed
races me to the clouds,
passing far away
from where my wife dwells.

O scarlet leaves
falling on the autumn mountainside:
stop, for a while, the storm
your strewing makes, that I might glimpse
the place where my wife dwells.

138

One version has for the first poem,

People may say that the Sea of Iwami,
having no harboring coves,
has no good inlets,
they may say it has no good lagoons,
but I don't care.
Though it has no good inlets,
I don't care.
Though it has no good lagoons,
the wind, when dawn comes,
and the waves, when evening descends,
carry over those whale-hunted seas
to the desolate beach in Nikita harbor
green, sleek seaweed,
seaweed from the offing,
and the memory of my wife's
well-woven sleeves,
there where I left her
  as mist and frost
    are left on the ground,
she who bent to my side in sleep
  like the sleek seaweed
swaying to and fro with the waves.

Though I look back ten thousand times
from each of this road's eighty bends,
my village has now receded
farther and farther in the distance.
Higher and higher
are the mountains I have crossed.
That I might gaze on the village of Tsuno

where my wife -
    ah, I love her! -
in her sighing
wilts like the summer grass,
mountains, bend down!

139

A variant envoy with this is,

I wonder if my wife
saw the sleeves I waved
from between the trees
on Utsuta Mountain
by the sea of Iwami.

140

*Poem by the maiden of Yosami, the wife of Kakinomoto
Hitomaro, upon parting from him*

"Do not worry," you say,
but I would cease my longing
only if I knew
when I shall meet you again.

LAMENTS

The Reign of Empress Saimei, Who Ruled the Realm Under Heaven from the Later Okamoto Palace (655-661)

141 and 142

Two poems by Prince Arima, written in his own sorrow as he tied the branches of a pine tree in a prayer for safety

I draw and tie together
   branches of the pine
      on the beach at Iwashiro.
If all goes well
I shall return to see them again.

The rice I would heap
   into a vessel
      if I were home—
since I journey,
   grass for pillow,
I heap into an oak leaf.

143 and 144

Two poems by Naga Okimaro, choked with sorrow
upon seeing the pine with its branches tied

I wonder if he
who tied the branches of the pine
on the cliff
     by Iwashiro's sea
returned to see them again.

The pine
standing in the fields of Iwashiro
with its branches tied:
and my heart is undone
as my thoughts turn to the past.

145

Poem written by Yamanoue Okura at a later time
responding to Okimaro's

Soaring like a bird
     across the sky,
he is present and he sees.
Men do not know it
but the pine must know.

> Although the above poems are not
> "laments,"—i.e., *banka* in the sense
> of "coffin-pulling poems," they share
> the same poetic intention, and
> therefore have been classified here
> with the Laments.

146

*Poem written upon seeing the pine tree with its branches
tied, at the time of the imperial procession to the land of
Ki in the first year of Taihō (701)*

> This poem is in the *Hitomaro
> Collection*

In hopes of later seeing them,
you tied the branches
of the young pine at Iwashiro.
Did you see its buds again?

THE REIGN OF EMPEROR TENJI, WHO RULED THE
REALM UNDER HEAVEN FROM THE ŌTSU PALACE IN
ŌMI (661-671)

147

*Poem presented by the Empress when the Emperor
was ill*

Turning to gaze
upon the fields of heaven,
I see my Lord's long life
stretch to fill the firmament.

148

*One book has the following poem, presented by the
Empress when the Emperor's illness suddenly took a
turn for the worse*

My eyes can see
your presence hovering
over Kohata,
    of the blue flags,
but I cannot meet you in the flesh.

149

Poem by the Empress upon the Emperor's death

People say, "Enough,
stop thinking of him,"
yet I cannot forget
while I see his image
in the wreath of jewels.

150

*Poem upon the death of the Emperor by one of his
concubines*

    Her name is yet unclear.

As the living are unfit
for commune with the gods,
so I am separated from you,
Lord whom I grieve for in the morning,
so I am kept from you,
Lord whom I long for.
If you were a jewel,

I would wrap you round my wrist.
If you were a robe,
I would never take you off.
Lord whom I long for,
last night I saw you
          in a dream.

151 and 152

*Two poems at the time of the Emperor's temporary
mausoleum*

If I had known
it would come to this,
I would have tied signs of interdiction
around the harbor
where the imperial craft did berth.

Does Cape Kara in Shiga
wait in longing
for the imperial craft
of our Lord, sovereign
of the earth's eight corners?

153

Poem by the Empress

Ships that come rowing
far on the offing,
ships that come rowing
close by the strand
on Ōmi's whale-hunted seas:
Oars on the offing,
do not splash so hard.
Oars by the strand,

do not splash so hard,
or the bird
  beloved of my husband,
who was gentle
  like the young grass,
will fly away.

154

Poem by the concubine of the Ishikawa family

For whom does the guardian
of Sasanami's imperial mountains
post there his signs of interdiction,
now that you, my Lord, are no longer?

155

*Poem by Princess Nukada when the mourners withdrew
from the Emperor's tomb and dispersed*

In awe they serve the tomb
of our Lord, sovereign
of the earth's eight corners,
on Kagami Mountain
in Yamashina.
There through the night,
    each night,
through the day,
    each day,
they have stayed,
weeping and crying aloud.
Now have the courtiers
of his great palace,
its ramparts thick with stone,
left and gone apart?

The Reign of Emperor Temmu, Who Ruled the Realm Under Heaven from the Kiyomihara Palace in Asuka (673-686)

156-158

Three poems by Crown Prince Takechi upon the death of Princess To'ochi

I see her only from afar,
for she is lofty
    like the divine cedar
        by the shrine at Mimoro.
Many are the nights I sleep alone.[3]

Short was her life
like the short mulberry,
    the true mulberry
        by Miwa Mountain,
though I thought it would be long.

I would go
draw the crystal waters
on the mountain
    decked with butterburs,
but I do not know the path.

> The *Nihonshoki* states that in
> summer, on the seventh day of the
> fourth month, in the seventh year of
> the reign (679), Princess Toochi
> suddenly became ill and died within
> the palace.

[3] The text here is corrupt, and this is only one of the many possible meanings of this poem.

159

Poem by the Empress upon the death of the Emperor

Scarlet leaves on Kami Hill
that our Lord, sovereign
of the earth's eight corners,
gazed on when evening came
and went to view when morning came—
if he were here
he would go view them today,
he would gaze on them tomorrow.
As I look back
upon that hill,
how sad I am when evening comes,
how desolate my days when morning comes!
The sleeves of my hempen robe
        are never dry.

160 and 161

One book has the following two poems by the present
Retired Empress (at that time the Empress) upon the
death of the Emperor

Do they not say
one can pluck a burning fire
and hold it in a sack?
So I summon the day
when I may meet my Lord.

The clouds,
   the blue clouds
trailing on the northern mountain
tear away from the stars,
      tear from the moon.

162

On the ninth day of the ninth month in the eighth year
after the Emperor's death (694), a Buddhist feast was
held in his memory. That night the following poem came
to the Empress in a dream.

> This poem is in *An Anthology of*
> *Ancient Poems.*

Our Lord, sovereign
of the earth's eight corners,
who ruled the realm under heaven
from the Kiyomihara Palace
     in Asuka,
child of the high-shining sun—
what could have been in his mind?
The land of Ise,
   of the divine wind,
is a land of brine-smacking waves
where toss the seaweed of the offing.
O so well did I love
the child of the high-shining sun!

THE REIGN OF EMPRESS JITŌ, WHO RULED THE REALM UNDER HEAVEN FROM THE FUJIWARA PALACE (686-697)

163 and 164

Two poems by Princess Ōku when, after the death of Prince Ōtsu, she came up from the Shrine of our offerings at Ise to the capital

For what have I come
when I might have stayed
in the land of Ise,
    of the divine wind?
For what,
now that you are no longer?

For what have I come
when you,
    whom I prayed to see,
        are no longer?
I have only tired my horse.

165 and 166

Two poems written by Princess Ōku in sorrow when they removed the remains of Prince Ōtsu to Futakami Mountain in Katsuragi

I who stay among the living
shall, from tomorrow,
look on Futakami Mountain
    as you, my brother.

I would pluck the andromeda
that grows on the beach,
but they say that you
are not here to look at it.

> The above poem does not seem to be
> about the removal of the Prince's
> remains. Perhaps it might have been
> written by the Princess sorrowing
> over the flowers by the road when
> she returned from the Ise Shrine to
> the capital.

167

*Poem by Kakinomoto Hitomaro at the time of the
temporary enshrinement of the Crown Prince, Peer of
the Sun*[4]

> with tanka

In the beginning
of heaven and earth,
on the riverbanks
of the far firmament,
the eight million deities,
the ten million deities
gathered in godly assembly
and held divine counsel,
and judged that the Sun Goddess,
      Amaterasu,
would rule the heavens
and, that he should rule
this land below,
where ears of rice flourish

---

[4] Crown Prince Kusakabe, who was meant to succeed his father, Emperor
Temmu, but died suddenly just before his enthronement.

on the reed plains,
until heaven and earth
draw together again,
pushed apart the eight-fold
clouds of heaven
and sent down to us
the high-shining Prince.
He ruled as a god
at the Kiyomi Palace
in Asuka,
   where the birds fly,
until he opened heaven's gate of stone
and rose, godlike, to those fields,
dwelling of Emperors.

If our Lord, the Crown Prince,
had lived to follow him
and rule the realm under heaven,
how, like the spring blossoms,
he would have been noble,
how, like the full moon,
he would have waxed great.
So the people
of the earth's four directions
placed their hopes on him,
   as on a great ship,
and looked up to him in expectation
as, in a drought,
   to the flood-swollen sky.
But—what could have been
in his mind?—
he has driven thick palace pillars
by remote Mayumi Hill
and raised high his mausoleum hall.
Now many days and months have passed

since the voice of his morning commandments
fell silent,
and the Prince's courtiers
do not know which way to turn.

168 and 169

Two envoys

That the palace
of the Prince I held in awe
as I would look up
to the far firmament
should fall to ruins—
alas!

The crimson-gleaming sun
still shines,
but that the moon is hidden
in the pitch-black night it crosses—
alas!

> In one book, these poems are envoys
> to a poem written at the time of the
> temporary enshrinement of a later
> Crown Prince.

170

One book has,

In the Garden Palace,
  in the Curved Pool,
the roaming water-birds
  long for men's eyes
and do not dive.

171-193

Twenty-three poems written by the servingmen at the
Palace of the Crown Prince in their sorrow

171

O the Garden Palace
where our child
    of the high-shining sun
was meant to rule the land
for ten thousand generations!

172

O roaming water-birds
   in the Garden Palace,
   in the Upper Pool,
do not wing away
   with wild fluttering,
even if our Lord is gone.

173

If our child
   of the high-shining sun
were here,
the Garden Palace halls
would not fall to ruin.

174

And Mayumi Hill,
   that I have looked on
      as a place of no concern:
Now it is the dwelling of our Lord,
so I shall stay there serving it
as his eternal palace halls.

175

Not even in my dreams
did I imagine this:
   with gloom, proceeding
      to his palace
on the bending road
      by Hinokuma.

176

I served him thinking,
   "until the end
      of heaven and earth."
My heart has been betrayed.

177

Gathering by Sata Hill
illumined by the rising sun,
the tears we cry
      know no ceasing.

178

When we looked
on the Garden where he stood,
our tears streamed down
   like sudden showers.
We could not hold them.

179

Though we do not tire
   of the Garden Palace
      at Tachibana,
must we go to Sata Hill
and stay there serving?

180

O birds who make your home
in the very Garden where he stood,
do not wing away
   with wild fluttering,
even if the year may change.

181

I look now on the jagged rocks
in the Garden where he stood:
are they not overgrown with grass
that did not grow before?

182

O young geese we raised
in nests we built for you
        with wooden stakes,
when you are ready to leave
come flying back to Mayumi Hill.

183

I, who had thought
our imperial halls
would flourish eternally,
        for a thousand ages—
how sad I am!

184

Though I wait on him
by the imperial Gate
where the eastern waters fall,
he will not summon me,
not today, not tomorrow.

185

Will I ever see again
that path of azaleas
        blooming,
spreading over stones
where the rocky poolside bends?

186

The great Eastern Gate
    that I passed through
        a thousand times a day
now I hesitate to enter.

187

If we return
to Sata's remote hillside,
who will reside
on the Garden steps?

188

Morning was overcast,
the sun did not come out,
so I came down to the Garden
and stayed here lamenting.

189

By the imperial halls in the Garden
    illumined by the rising sun
there was not the slightest rustle of men,
and in my heart was sorrow.

190

Stout was my heart
like pillars of thick pine,
but now this heart
    cannot be assuaged.

191

Will the great fields of Uda
    be remembered,
where he went on procession,
with stores of woolen clothes
for winter and for spring?

192

Like the birds that cry
    on Sata's hillside
    illumined by the rising sun,
I have cried each evening of this year.

193

I shall take the road
the ploughhands tread
  both day and night
for my daily path to his palace.

      The *Nihonshoki* records the Crown
      Prince's death in summer, on the
      thirteenth day of the fourth month, in
      the third year of the reign (689).

194

Poem presented by Kakinomoto Hitomaro to Princess
Hatsusebe and Prince Osakabe

with tanka

Sleek seaweed streams
from where it grows
on the upper shallows of the Asuka,
            where the birds fly,
to touch and touch again
the lower shoals.

                Asleep
without the folds of his wife's
soft skin,
        that once he kept beside him
            like his swords,
when she, like sleek seaweed,
bent toward him, swaying to and fro—
now desolate lies the bed
of his pitch-black nights.

So, inconsolate, yet hoping
she might meet him,
she sojourns,
            grass for pillow,
on the broad, jewel-trailed fields of Ochi,
her pearly hems muddied in morning dew,
her robe drenched in evening mist,
for the Prince she cannot meet again.

195

Envoy

The Prince who crossed the sleeves
of his evening robe with hers
has passed beyond the jewel-trailed
fields of Ochi. How could she hope
to meet him again?

> One book states that the above
> poems were presented to Princess
> Hatsusebe when Prince Kawashima
> was buried on the fields of Ochi. The
> *Nihonshoki* records that Prince
> Kawashima, of Jōdaisan Rank, died
> in autumn, on the ninth day of the
> ninth month, in the fifth year of
> Akamitori (691).

196

*Poem by Kakinomoto Hitomaro at the time of the
temporary enshrinement of Princess Asuka at Kinoe*

> with tanka

On the upper shallows
of the Asuka,
     where the birds fly,
they have made a bridge of stepping stones.
Over the lower shallows
they have placed a temporary bridge of wood.
The sleek seaweed
trailing on the bridge of stones
may be broken, but still it grows.
The riverweed
spreading on the wooden bridge

may wither, but still it sprouts.
Why, then, does our Princess
leave her splendid Lord,
who bent toward her
when she stood like sleek seaweed
or lay like riverweed?
Does she forget his morning palace?
Does she turn her back on his evening palace?

While in this world,
she would sometimes go on excursions
to the palace at Kinoe,
   where the plates face each other
   on the feasting trays,
with her splendid Lord,
who brought her blossoms in springtime
to decorate her hair
and, when autumn came,
garlanded her with yellow leaves,
who lined his well-woven sleeves with hers,
who was a mirror she did not tire to gaze on,
whom she praised as the moon waxing to fullness.
Now she has fixed that palace
as her eternal shrine.
Gone are the eyes he was met with,
lapsed the words spoken to him.

That must be why our Prince,
choked with sorrow,
moaning his unrequited love
like the tiger thrush,
goes back and forth,
like the morning birds,
to attend her.
When we see him

wilting
like the summer grass,
staggering
like an evening star,
reeling
like a great boat,
we cannot console ourselves,
we do not know what to do.
At least let us remember,
if only the sound,
      if only the name,
forever far and long
as heaven and earth.
Ten thousand ages
to the Asuka River
that bears the name
of our beloved Princess:
      her memento,
it is here.

197 and 198

Tanka

If they had piled branches
across the Asuka River
to stop its course,
even the streaming waters
would have become quiet.

Asuka, river of
      "tomorrow's fragrance":
hoping, but in vain, to meet her
at least tomorrow, I cannot forget
my Princess' name.

199

*Poem by Kakinomoto Hitomaro at the time of the
temporary enshrinement of Prince Takechi at Kinoe*

with tanka

I hesitate to put it in words,
it is an awesome thing to speak.
Our Lord,
who, while we trembled,
fixed the far and heavenly
halls of his shrine
on the fields of Makami in Asuka
and, godlike, has secluded himself
                    in the rocks there,
he,
who ruled the earth's eight corners,
crossed Fuwa Mountain,
lined with thick black pines,
in the northern land of his realm
and went down,
        as from heaven,
            to the provinces,
encamping on the plain of Wazami,
    Wazami
            of the Korean swords.
To hold sway over the realm under heaven
and bring his dominions to peace,
he gathered his soldiers
in the eastern country,
        where the cock cries,
and gave the task to his son,
he being an imperial prince:

to pacify the raging rebels
and subdue the defiant lands.

Then our Prince
girded his great body with his long sword
and took in his great hands his bow.
The sound of the drums,
calling the troops to ready,
boomed like the very voice of thunder,
and the echoing notes
of the signaller's flute
grew, to the terror of all,
like the roar of a tiger
with prey in its eyes.
The rippling of the high-held banners
was like the rippling of the fires
struck across every field
when spring comes, bursting winter's bonds,
and the roar of the bowstrings they plucked
was so fearful, we thought it a hurricane
whirling through a snowfallen winter forest.
When the arrows they let loose
swarmed like a blinding swirl of snow,
the resisters, standing defiant,
also resolved to perish,
                    if they must,
like the dew and frost.
As they struggled
    like zooming birds,
the divine wind
from the Shrine of our offerings
at Ise in Watarai
blew confusion upon them,
hiding the very light of day

as clouds blanketed the heavens
in eternal darkness.

Thus pacifying this land,
abundant in ears of rice,
our Lord, sovereign
of the earth's eight corners,
          a very god,
firmly drove his palace pillars
and proclaimed his rule
over the realm under heaven—
for ten thousand generations,
          we thought.
But just as his reign flourished
brilliant as the white bouquets
          of mulberry paper,
suddenly they deck his princely halls
to make a godly shrine,
and the courtiers who served him
now wear mourning clothes of white hemp.
On the fields
before the Haniyasu Palace gate
they crawl and stumble like deer
as long as the sun still streams its crimson,
and when pitch-black night descends
they crawl around like quail,
turning to look up at the great halls.
They wait upon him,
but they wait in vain,
and so they moan
like the plaintive birds of spring.
Before their cries can be stilled
or their mournful thoughts exhausted
the divine cortege
is borne from the Kudara Plain,

borne away.
Loftily he raises
the palace at Kinoe,
    good of hempen cloth,
as his eternal shrine.
A god, his soul is stilled there.
Yet could we even imagine
that his palace by Kagu Hill
        will pass away
in the ten thousand generations
he intended as he built?
I turn to gaze on it
as I would on the heavens,
bearing it in my heart
    like a strand of jewels,
preciously remembering,
awesome though it be.

200 and 201

Envoys

Although you rule
the far heavens now,
we go on longing for you,
unmindful of the passing
of sun and moon.

Not knowing where they will drift,
like the hidden puddles that run
on the banks of Haniyasu Pond,
the servingmen stand bewildered.

202

One book has for an envoy,

Offering him sacred wine,
we pray at the shrine of Nakisawa,
    the marsh of tears.
But our Lord is gone
to rule the high heavens.

> In the *Forest of Classified Verse*, the
> above poem is said to be "by Princess
> Hinokuma, in her anger at the
> Nakisawa Shrine (for the Prince's
> absence)." The *Nihonshoki* states
> that the later Crown Prince, Takechi,
> died in autumn, on the tenth day of
> the seventh month, in the tenth year
> of the reign (696).

203

*Poem by Prince Hozumi crying in sorrow on a winter
day after the death of Princess Tajima, as he looked out
through the falling snow toward her grave*

Falling snow,
    do not fall so hard.
Do not be a barrier to my sight
of Ikai Hill in Yonabari.

204

Poem by Okisome Azumabito upon the death of Prince Yuge

with tanka

Our Lord, who ruled
in peace,
our child
of the high-shining sun,
a very god,
dwells as a divinity
in the far heavenly palace.
So with awe
we fall before him
and lament through the day,
      each day,
and through the night,
      each night,
but cannot cry enough.

205

Envoy

Our Lord,
a very god,
conceals himself
behind five hundred
folds of cloud.

206

Another envoy

Like the rippling, rippling
     of the tiny waves
at Sasanami in Shiga,
so did we always
think of our Lord.

207-212

*Two poems by Kakinomoto Hitomaro as he shed tears
of blood in his grief following the death of his wife*

     with tanka

207

I.

On the Karu Road[5]
is the village of my wife,
and I desired to meet her intimately,
but if I went there too much
the eyes of others would cluster around us,
and if I went there too often
others would find us out.
And so I hoped
that later we would meet
like tangling vines,
trusted that we would
as I would trust a great ship,

---

[5] "Karu" is preceded by the formal epithet *ama tobu ya*, "that soars through
the sky," a pun on the word "*karu*" in its sense of "light" or "buoyant." Like
the pillow-word "*koto saeku*" which preceded the name "Cape Kara" in
poem no. 135 (see note 2 above), it is essentially untranslatable.

and hid my love:
faint as jewel's light,
a pool walled in by cliffs.

Then came the messenger,
        his letter tied
        to a jewelled catalpa twig,
to tell me,
        in a voice
        like the sound
        of a catalpa bow,
that my girl,
who had swayed to me in sleep
like seaweed of the offing,
was gone
like the coursing sun
gliding into dusk,
like the radiant moon
secluding itself behind the clouds,
gone like the scarlet leaves of autumn.

I did not know what to say,
                what to do,
but simply could not listen
and so, perhaps to solace
a single thousandth
    of my thousand-folded longing,
I stood at the Karu market
where often she had gone,
and listened,
but could not even hear
the voices of the birds
that cry on Unebi Mountain,
    where the maidens
        wear strands of jewels,

and of the ones who passed me
on that road,
    straight as a jade spear,
not one resembled her.
I could do nothing
but call my wife's name
and wave my sleeves.

208 and 209

Envoys

Too dense the yellowed leaves
on the autumn mountain:
my wife is lost
and I do not know the path
to find her by.

With the falling away
of the yellowed leaves,
I see the messenger
with his jewelled catalpa staff,
and I recall the days I met her.

210

II.

She was my wife,
to whom my thoughts gathered
thick as the spring leaves
spreading from the myriad branches
of the zelkova tree
on the embankment (a quick run
from her gate),

that we would pick
and look at together
while she was of this world.
She was the girl I depended on
but now, unable to break
the course of this world,
she shrouds herself from me
in heavenly white raiments
on a withered, sun-simmered plain
and rises away in the morning
like a bird
and conceals herself
like the setting sun.

Each time our infant,
the memento she left,
cries out in hunger,
I, though a man,
having nothing to give it,
hug it to my breast.
Inside the wedding house
where the pillows we slept on
lie pushed together,
I live through the days
desolate and lonely
and sigh through the nights.
Lament as I may,
I know nothing I can do.
Long for her as I may,
I have no way to meet her,
and so when someone said,
"She dwells on Hagai Mountain,
        of the great bird,"
I struggled up here,
kicking the rocks apart,

but it did no good:
my wife, whom I thought
was of this world,
is less visible
than the faint light of a jewel.

211 and 212

Tanka

The autumn moon shines
as it did when I watched last year,
but my wife, who watched with me—
the drift of the year has taken her.

Leaving my wife on Hikide Mountain
by the Fusuma Road,
I come down the mountain path,
hardly alive.

213

A variant has,

She was my wife,
to whom my thoughts gathered
thick as the spring leaves,
like the myriad branches budding
on the zelkova tree
on the embankment (a short step
from her gate),
that we would bring
and look at together
while she was of this world.
She was my wife,
on whom I depended,

but now, unable to break
the course of this world,
she shrouds herself from me
in heavenly white raiments
on a withered, sun-simmered plain,
and rises away in the morning
like a bird,
and conceals herself
like the setting sun.

Each time our infant,
the memento she left,
cries out in hunger,
I, though a man,
having nothing to give it,
hug it to my breast.
Inside the wedding house
where the pillows we slept on
lie pushed together,
I live through the days
desolate and lonely
and sigh through the nights.
Lament as I may,
I know nothing I can do.
Long for her as I may,
I have no way to meet her.
And so when someone said,
"The wife you long for
dwells on Hagai Mountain,
        of the great bird,"
I struggled up here,
kicking the rocks apart,
but it did no good:
my wife, whom I thought
was of this world,
is ash.

214-216

Envoys

The autumn moon crosses the heavens
as it did when I watched last year,
but my wife, who watched with me—
the drift of the year has taken her.

Leaving my wife on Hikide Mountain
by the Fusuma Road,
I think of the path she has taken,
and I am hardly alive.

I come home
and gaze inside:
facing outward
on the haunted floor,
my wife's boxwood pillow.

217

*Poem by Kakinomoto Hitomaro upon the death of the
maiden of Tsu in Kibi*

　　with tanka

Wife beautiful
as the reddened autumn hills,
girl lithe
as soft bamboo,
what could have been in her mind?
Life long as mulberry rope—
only if it were dew,
then we could say
that, rising in the morning,

it vanishes by evening.
Only if it were mist,
then we could say
that, rising in the morning,
it is lost by morning.
But even I,
    who only heard of her
        like the sound
        of a catalpa bow,
regret I saw her only faintly.
Her husband, young
            like the spring grass,
who was pillowed
in her finely-clothed arms,
who, when he slept,
kept her beside him
            like his swords:
is it loneliness
that keeps him thinking of her,
and from sleep?
Is it regret
that keeps him thinking of her,
and longing?
Girl who has gone
before her time,
like dew in the morning,
like mist in the evening.

218 and 219

Tanka

Gazing on the road
  by the river shallows,
for the girl of Tsu, in Shiga
  of the rippling waves,
the road of death—
what loneliness!

When I met the girl
of Ōtsu—like the sky
  in its vastness—
I saw her only faintly.
        Now,
now I regret it!

220

*Poem by Kakinomoto Hitomaro upon seeing a dead man
lying among the rocks on the island of Samine in Sanuki*

  with tanka

The land of Sanuki,
  fine in sleek seaweed:
is it for the beauty of the land
that we do not tire
  to gaze upon it?
Is it for its divinity
that we deem it most noble?
Eternally flourishing,
    with the heavens
        and the earth,
    with the sun
        and the moon,

the very face of a god—
so it has come down
        through the ages.

Casting off
from Naka harbor,
we came rowing.
Then tide winds
blew through the clouds;
on the offing
we saw the rustled waves,
on the strand
we saw the roaring crests.
Fearing the whale-hunted seas,
our ship plunged through—
we bent those oars!
Many were the islands
near and far,
but we beached on Samine—
        beautiful its name—
and built a shelter
        on the rugged shore.

Looking around,
            we saw you
lying there
on a jagged bed of stones,
the beach
        for your finely woven pillow,
by the breakers' roar.
        If I knew your home,
I would go and tell them.
If your wife knew,

she would come and seek you out.
But she does not even know the road,
        straight as a jade spear.
Does she not wait for you,
        worrying and longing,
your beloved wife?

221 and 222

Envoys

If your wife were here,
she would gather and feed you
the starwort that grows
on the Sami hillsides,
but is its season not past?

Making a finely woven pillow
of the rocky shore
        where waves from the offing
                draw near,
you, who sleep there!

223

*Poem written by Kakinomoto Hitomaro in his own
sorrow as he was about to die in the land of Iwami*

Not knowing I am pillowed
among the crags on Kamo Mountain,
my wife must still be waiting
        for my return.

224 and 225

Two poems upon the death of Kakinomoto Hitomaro by his wife, the maiden of Yosami

Today, today!
Each day I have waited for you,
and now do they not say
you are strewn with the shells
              of Ishi River?

Never again to meet him
              in the flesh—
Rise, o clouds, and spread
over Ishi River,
that, gazing on you,
I may remember him.

226

Poem by Tajihi Mahito answering her with Hitomaro's supposed feelings

Who will tell you
that I lie pillowed here
beside the gems tossed ashore
in the surging waves?

227

A variant has,

Leaving you on a desolate plain
in a barbarous place
at the far reach of the heavens,
I still go on thinking of you,
and I am hardly alive.

> The name of the author of the above
> poem is not yet clear. But in the old
> book it is placed here.

THE ERA OF THE NARA PALACE (710-784)

228 and 229

*In the fourth year of Wadō (711), Kawabe Miyahito
found a young girl's corpse in a field of pines at
Himejima, and wrote these two poems in his sorrow.*

Let my girl's name
stream on through a thousand ages,
until moss grows
on the buds of the young pine
        at Himejima.

O tides in Naniwa lagoon,
I pray you do not ebb,
for it would pain me
to see the body of the young girl
sunken in the sea.

230

Poem upon the death of Prince Shiki in the ninth month,
autumn, of the first year of Reiki (715)

   with tanka

Takamato[6] is round
like the targets brave men face
when they take up catalpa bows
and squeeze in their fingers
beast-subduing arrows.
"What flames are those?" I asked,
what flames burning, bright
as field-fires on the spring plains,
by Takamato Mountain?
One who came walking on that road
     straight as a jade spear
stopped, and with tears that fell
        like drizzling rain,
        drenching his white garments,
spoke to me:
"Why must you ask such a thing?
If you ask me,
     I shall cry out in my weeping.
If I speak it,
     it will pain my heart.
It is the torches they carry
in the funeral procession
of the Emperor's son
that make a profusion of light."

---

[6] The expression in the first five lines of this poem is based on a pun on the name "Takamato." The *"mato"* in Takamato is also a "target" (的 *mato*). The same device is used in poem no. 61 (see Book One, note 8 above).

231 and 232

Tanka

Autumn bush clover
on the Takamato fields,
do you bloom and fall in vain,
though the one who would gaze on you
is gone?

Is the road through the fields
by Mikasa Mountain
so very overgrown
with withered grass?
But he has not been gone so long.

> The above poems are in the *Kasa
> Kanamura Collection.*

233 and 234

A variant has for the tanka,

Autumn bush clover
on the Takamato fields,
do not fall,
for I would gaze on you
as a memento
and think of our Lord.

Oh is the road that comes
from the fields by Mikasa Mountain
so very overgrown
with withered grass?
But he has not been gone so long.

BOOK THREE

The Inland Sea

Gazing on the channel
where they ply back and forth
to our Lord's distant Court,
I think of the age of the gods.

> Kakinomoto Hitomaro (one of "Two poems while he was
> travelling by sea down to the land of Tsukushi," III.304)

POEMS ON VARIOUS THEMES

235

Poem written by Kakinomoto Hitomaro at the time of the Empress' excursion to Ikazuchi Hill, "the hill of thunder"

Our Lord,
a very god,
builds her lodge
above the thunder
by the heavenly clouds.

> A variant of the above poem has it
> dedicated to Prince Osakabe. The
> variant reads,
>
> > Our Lord,
> > a very god,
> > spreads his palace precincts
> > on the hill of thunder,
> > hidden in the clouds.

236

Poem given by the Empress to the old woman Shihi

Lately I do not hear
the talk that Shihi forces on me,
though I tell her, "Stop!",
and now I long for it.

237

Poem presented by the old woman Shihi in response

> The woman's personal name is yet
> unclear.

Though I say, "I want to stop,"
you command me, "Speak! Speak!"
So Shihi speaks, and then you say
I force it on you!

238

Poem by Naga Okimaro, composed in response to an
imperial command

It sounds into the inner precincts
of the great palace:
the fisherman's cry
as he leads the net boys
hauling in the nets.

239

Poem written by Kakinomoto Hitomaro at the time of
Prince Naga's excursion to Kariji Pond

> with envoys

Our Lord, sovereign
of the earth's eight corners,
our child of the high-shining sun,
lines his steeds
and sets out on the royal hunt.
On the fields of Kariji,
   on his hunting trail
among the slender rushes,

the boar and deer
crawl prostrate to behold him,
the very quail
crawl on the ground around him.
Like the boar and deer,
we crawl prostrate to behold him,
like the quail,
we crawl on the ground around him.
In awe, we serve him.
However much we look upon him
as we would gaze on a true clear mirror,
      gaze with eyes that see
           the far firmament,
he is, like the spring grasses,
ever more precious,
our Lord.

240

Envoy

Catching in a net
   the moon in its course
      down the far firmament,
our Lord makes it the canopy
of his silk umbrella.

    A variant has,

      Our Lord,
      a very god,
      constructs a sea
      among the crags
      where tower thick black pines.

242

Poem by Prince Yuge at the time of his excursion to Yoshino

I dare not think
I shall last eternally
like the clouds
    on Mifune Mountain
       above the rapids.

243

Poem presented by Prince Kasuga in response

Our Lord shall be
for a thousand years.
Will there ever come a day
when the white clouds vanish
from Mifune Mountain?

244

A variant (on 242) has,

I dare not think
I shall last eternally
like the clouds that rise
    on Mifune Mountain
    in splendid Yoshino.

    The above poem is in the
    Kakinomoto Hitomaro Collection.

245 and 246

*Two poems by Prince Nagata when he crossed to Mizu
Island on his way to Tsukushi on imperial orders*

Just as I have heard,
it is truly noble
and wierdly enspirited,
this island of Mizu.

We would set our ship
out from Nosaka Cove
    in Ashikita
and sail to Mizu Island.
Waves, do not rise!

247

Poem by Lord Ishikawa in response

    His personal name is lost.

Though waves rise on the offing
    and on the shore,
the wave shall not rise
that can stop my man's royal ship.

    Present investigation shows that there
    was a Lord Ishikawa Miyamaro, of
    lesser Sub-Fourth Rank, who was
    Administrator of the Dazaifu during
    the Kyō'un Period (704-707), and
    also a Lord Ishikawa Kimiko, of
    lesser Full Fifth Rank, who was a
    Vice-Commander of the Dazaifu
    during the Jinki Period (724-728). We
    do not know which of these two
    wrote this poem.

248

Another poem by Prince Nagata

Today I saw the Satsuma Channel,
    Satsuma
        of the wild Hayato men,
distant as the dwelling of the clouds.

249-256

Eight poems of travel by Kakinomoto Hitomaro

249

Fearing the billows
off Cape Mitsu,
you have passed the night by the island
on your boat in the hidden cove.[1]

250

Passing Minume,
where they cut the sleek seaweed,
our boat has drawn near Cape Noshima,
rank with summer grass.

    A variant has,

    Passing Otome,
    where they cut the sleek seaweed,
    I build my temporary lodge
    on Cape Noshima,
    rank with summer grass.

[1] This translation is based on a reading of the last two phrases of the
original poem as *funa naru kimi wa / yadorinu shima ni*, one of a dozen possible
readings of the obscure characters 舟公宣奴嶋尒.

251

At Cape Noshima in Awaji,
the cords of my sleeves
that my wife tied for me
are blown backward in the beach wind.

252

Do they see me as a fisher
catching perch in Fujie Cove,
    of the hempen cloth,
I who journey?

    A variant has,

        Do they see me as a fisher
        angling in Fujie Cove,
            of the white cloth,
        I who journey?

253

Even as I think how hard it is
to leave behind the fields of Inabi,
the island of Kago,
    for which my heart yearns,
        comes into sight.

254

Will I part rowing to the sun
that sinks into the Akashi Straits,
    bright with lampfires,
the land of home beyond my sight?

255

Over a long road,
from barbarian lands
at the far reach of the heavens,
I have come, yearning.
And now the Straits of Akashi
open on the island, Yamato.

A variant has,

open on the land of my home

256

The surface of the sea at Kehi
looks peaceful; I can see,
bobbling out in confusion
like rushes scythed from roots,
the boats of fishermen.

A variant has,

The surface of the sea at Muko
looks peaceful; I can see,
above the waves,
the boats of angling fishermen.

257

Poem about Kagu Hill by Lord Kamo Tarihito

with tanka

When spring comes,
with rising mists,

to heavenly Kagu Hill,
  descended
  from the firmament,
the wind in the pines
raises waves on the pond,
and darkening leaves
thicken on the cherry trees.
On the offing
the lone duck cries for its mate,
by the shore
the spotted ducks flock and rustle.
Courtiers of the great palace,
    its ramparts
      thick with stone,
have taken their leave;
oars and poles
are gone from the boats,
and it is lonely,
with no one there to row them.

258 and 259

Two envoys

And I can clearly see
that the boats lie unrowed,
for the diving mandarin and the teal
have made them their home.

When did Kagu's halberd cedar
turn so venerably aged
that moss spreads on its roots?

260

A variant has (for 257),

When spring comes,
　with swaying branches,
to heavenly Kagu Hill,
　descended
　from the firmament,
darkening leaves
thicken on the cherry trees,
and the wind in the pines
lifts waves on the pond.
By the shore
the spotted ducks flock and rustle,
on the offing
the lone duck cries for its mate.
Courtiers of the great palace,
　　its ramparts
　　　thick with stone,
have taken their leave;
the oars and poles
are gone from the boats they rowed,
and it is lonely,
though I would row them.

261

*Poem presented by Kakinomoto Hitomaro to Prince
Niitabe*

　　with tanka

Our Lord, sovereign
of the earth's eight corners,
child of the high-shining sun—

May I make my way to him
       like the snow
coursing through the far firmament
to fall upon the great halls
where his reign flourishes,
there to attend him
as the years pass to eternity.

262

Envoy

Through the streaming snow
that hides the grove of trees
on Yatsuri Hill,
racing my steed to his halls:
the mornings are my delight.

263

*Poem by Osakabe Tarimaro when he came up to the
capital from the land of Ōmi*

I do not have days at my leisure
to see this land of Shiga,
but do not whip the horses harshly,
do not hasten me more.

264

*Poem by Kakinomoto Hitomaro when he reached the
banks of the Uji River on his way back to the capital
from the land of Ōmi*

Like the waves that wander
among the fishing stakes
in Uji River,
   of the eighty warrior clans,
I do not know which way to turn.

265

Poem by Naga Okimaro

How troublesome the falling rain:
here at the Sano Ford
      on Cape Miwa
there is no house for shelter.

266

Poem by Kakinomoto Hitomaro

Plover skimming evening waves
on the Ōmi Sea,
when you cry
         so my heart trails
like dwarf bamboo
      down to the past.

267

Poem by Prince Shiki

The flying squirrel,
seeking the furthest branch,
came across the hunter
of the foothill-trailing mountain!

268

Poem by Prince Nagaya on the native village

In Asuka,
village of my man's old home,
the plover is crying,
unable to find the garden.

> Present consideration suggests that
> this poem might have been written
> when the capital was moved from
> Asuka to the Fujiwara Palace.

269

Poem by Lady Abe about the Yabe Slope

If others did not notice,
I would have wrapped the fire in my sleeves
              and hidden it with me.
But I have not come in my sleeves,
and it must still be burning.[2]

---

[2] This poem apparently refers to the burning of the Yabe Slope, using it as
a metaphor for the fire of human passion. Yet the exact nature of that passion
is unclear; this is perhaps the reason why it is classified under the "poems on
various themes" rather than the "personal exchanges."

270-277

Eight poems of travel by Takechi Kurohito

270

Journeying, I fall into longing
                    over things,
and yet below the mountain
the red ship painted with clay
is rowed to the distant offing.

271

The cranes sweep, crying,
                to Sakurada;
it seems the tide has ebbed
                from Ayuchi Lagoon,
and the cranes sweep, crying.

272

Crossing over Shihatsu Mountain,
I look down:
    a tiny boat,
                with no gunwales,
is rowed away from Kasanui Island.

273

I have rowed around the rocky cape,
and now, on the Ōmi Sea,
            at Yaso Harbor,
the cranes flock and cry.

274

Row my boat to Hira Harbor,
I will sojourn there.
Do not leave for the offing.
The night has deepened.

275

Where shall I seek shelter?
On the Kachino Plain
          in Takashima
this sun is setting.

276

Is it because
my girl and I are one
that we cannot part
on two-forked Futami Road
in Mikawa, land of the three rivers?

> One book has,

> > We part on two-forked Futami Road
> > in Mikawa, land of the three rivers,
> > and my man and I are both alone.

277

I should have come sooner to see;
now the leaves of the clustered zelkovas
          at Taka in Yamashiro
lie scattered on the ground.

278

Poem by the youth Ishikawa

The fisherwomen of Shiga,
    cutting seaweed
    and burning salt,
have no time to take combs
    to their hair.

> Present consideration shows the
> above poet to be the son of Lord
> Ishikawa, called "Young Boy
> Ishikawa."

279 and 280

Two poems by Takechi Kurohito

I have shown my girl the Ina Plain.
When will I show her Nazusa Mountain,
and Matsubara in Tsuno?

Come lads,
make speed for Yamato!
Let us return with branches
we snap from the alder fields of Mano
where the white sedge grows.

281

Poem by Kurohito's wife in response

The alder fields of Mano
are seen by you
when you come and when you go
through those alder fields of Mano,
where the white sedge grows.

282

Poem by Kasuga Oyu

We have yet to pass Iware,
    where the vines
        crawl on the rocks.
When will we cross Hatsuse Mountain?
The night is deepening.

283

Poem by Takechi Kurohito

I stand in Ena Harbor
    in Suminoe
and look out:
    the boatmen casting off
    from the anchorage at Muko.

284

Poem by Kasuga Oyu

Oh, that girl I met
on the Abe market road
  in Suruga
when I was going to Yaki Harbor!

285

Poem by Tajihi Kasamaro when he passed over Se Mountain on his way to the land of Ki

I would speak my wife's name,
   trailing it
   like a scarf of mulberry.
How would it be if I hung her name
   on Se Mountain,
    "Husband's Mountain"?

286

Poem by Kasuga Oyu in immediate response

It is fit that my man
should bear the name
of Se Mountain,
   "Husband's Mountain."
Let us not call it "wife."

287

Poem by Lord Isonokami during the procession to Shiga

   His personal name is lost.

Where is my home,
now that I am here?
I have come over the mountain
where the white clouds trail.

288

Poem by Hozumi Oyu

If my life be safe,
let me see these once more:
the white waves cresting
to Ōtsu in Shiga.

> Present investigation has yet to clarify
> the year and month of the above
> procession.

289 and 290

Two poems on the crescent moon by Hashihito Ōura

Looking back
on the fields of heaven,
I see the moon suspended
like a drawn white bow,
 a true bow;
the night road should be safe.

Is it for the height
 of Kurahashi Mountain
that the moon's light is wan
as it emerges
 from the depths of night?

291

Poem about Se Mountain by Oda Tsukau

I have crossed Se Mountain
without stopping to admire
the black pines'
    thickly trailing leaves,
but the leaves knew
    that I must hurry.

292-295

Four poems by Tsuno Maro

292

The boat of stone,
    in which rode Sagume,
    goddess from the far firmament,
found anchorage in Taka Harbor;
now it has turned shallow.[3]

293

Now that the tide has ebbed
    from Mizu Harbor,
the fisherwomen must be out
with their sacks of sedge,
gathering the sleek seaweed.
Let us go now, and watch.

---

[3] The *Kojiki* records the myth of "Ama no Sagume," and the Tsu *Fudōki* (as mentioned in the *Zoku Karin Ryozaishū*) speaks of her journey, following her descent from the heavens, in a "heavenly boat of stone" which anchored at "Taka harbor."

294

The wind is quick,
and the white waves on the offing
must be high:
    the fishers' boats
        have returned to the beach.

295

Matsubara, the field of pines
   at Nogi in Suminoe,
is where our Lord,
    that distant god,
came on procession.

296 and 297

*Two poems by Lord Taguchi Masuhito when, on his
way to assume the governorship of the land of
Kamitsuke, he passed Cape Kiyomi in Suruga*

As I look out
on the vast expanse of water
in Miho Bay
   by Cape Kiyomi
   in Iohara,
I am free of all concern.

Tago Bay,
that I do not tire to look on
during the day—
now, in awe of my Lord's command,
I have looked on it at night.

298

Poem by Benki

Crossing Matsuchi Mountain at dusk,
I fear that I must sleep alone
on the banks of the Sumida River.

> One source states that Benki was the
> monastic name of Kasuga Oyu.

299

Poem by the Chancellor, Lord Ōtomo

> Which Lord Ōtomo is yet unclear.

I would regret it if the snow
pushing down on the sedge leaves
    in the inland mountains
were to melt away.
Rain, do not fall.

300 and 301

*Two poems by Prince Nagaya when he halted his steed
on Nara Mountain*

Passing Saho
and reaching the top of the Nara Slope,
I leave paper prayer strips there:
so that my wife and I may always meet,
my eyes never apart from hers.

Unable to cross the mountain
strewn with jagged rocks,
I may weep and cry aloud
but my face will not reveal
my longing for her.

302

Poem by the Councillor Lord Abe Hironiwa

There is still a little distance
        to my girl's home.
Can I beat the moon there
before it starts to cross
the pitch-black night?

303 and 304

*Two poems by Kakinomoto Hitomaro while he was
travelling by sea down to the land of Tsukushi*

On the offing
        of the Inami Sea—
                beautiful its name—
hidden by a thousand lapping waves,
the island, Yamato.

Gazing on the channel
where they ply back and forth
to our Lord's distant Court,
I think of the age of the gods.[4]

---

[4] This appears to refer not to any single myth, but rather to a sense of
grandeur which for Hitomaro is an attribute of "the age of the gods" itself.

305

Poem by Takechi Kurohito about the ruined capital at Ōmi

I swore not to see it,
  for I knew
   it would be like this.
But you have forced me to look
on Sasanami's ruined capital.

> One source states that the above
> poem is by Shoben. The facts about
> this Shoben are yet unclear.

306

Poem by Prince Aki during his procession to Ise

Would that the white waves
on the offing in the Ise Sea
    were flowers—
I would wrap them as souvenirs
and take them home to my wife.

307-309

Three poems by Prince Hakutsū when he viewed the caverns at Miho during a journey to the land of Ki

The caverns at Miho,
Miho of the pampas grass,
where dwelled the Kume youth—
though I gaze on them,
I do not tire.[5]

---

[5] This and the following two poems are apparently informed by an oral legend of the "Kume youth," i.e. the young man of the Kume clan; the legend is now lost.

Caverns, that last an eternity,
are still here even now,
but the men who dwelled in them
could not live forever.

O pine that stands
  at the caverns' entrance,
looking at you
    is like coming face to face
    with the men of ancient times.

310

*Poem by Prince Kadobe about the tree at the Eastern
market*

It has been long since we met,
long as it takes the tree
planted at the Eastern market
to grow thick foliage.
I have reason to yearn.

311

*Poem by Kuratsukuri Masuhito when he came up to the
capital from the land of Buzen*

It has been long
since I have seen Kagami Mountain
    in the land of Toyo,[6]
    where the catalpa bow
    echoes when shot,
and so I yearn for it.

---

[6] Buzen is the "front" land of Toyo ("*Toyokuni no michi no kuchi*"). In the
poem this is simply "*Toyokuni*", the entire land of Toyo.

312

Poem by the Minister of Ceremonies, Lord Fujiwara Umakai, at the time when, under imperial orders, he built the new palace at Naniwa.

In the old days they called it
rustic Naniwa. But now
that we have moved our palace here,
how like a capital it's become!

313

Poem by Tori Senryō

O white waves cresting in the rapids
            at splendid Yoshino,
though I do not know the ancient times
they have been told of
        down through the generations,
and my thoughts turn to the past.

314

Poem by Hata Otari

On the way to Koshi,
    where rippling waves
    cross the beaches,
runs the river Notose—
the clarity of its sound
in every rapid shoal!

315

*Poem by the Councillor, Lord Ōtomo Tabito, written in
response to an imperial command, during the procession
to the detached palace at Yoshino in the late spring*

> With tanka; these poems were not
> recited at the time.

It seems the mountains
around the palace
  at splendid Yoshino
make it noble,
it seems the river
makes it bright and clear.
Let it endure,
    forever unchanging,
        as long as heaven and earth,
for ten thousand years—
the palace of our Lord's procession.

316

Envoy

Gazing now
on the stream at Kisa
that I gazed on in the past,
I see how, more and more,
it has become bright and clear.

317

Poem on viewing Mount Fuji by Yamabe Akahito

with tanka

Since the time
when heaven and earth split apart,
Fuji's lofty peak
has stood in the land of Suruga,
    high and noble,
    like a very god.

As I gaze up to it
through the fields of heaven,
I see it hides the light
of the sky-traversing sun,
and the very gleam of the moon
is invisible in its shadow.
It thwarts the white clouds
    from their path,
and snow falls on its summit
outside the bounds of time.
Let us speak of it
and recount it to the ages—
Fuji's lofty peak!

318

Envoy

Coming out
    from Tago's nestled cove,
I gaze:
    white, pure white
the snow has fallen
on Fuji's lofty peak.

319

Poem about Mount Fuji

Rising between the lands of Kai
and Suruga,
   where the waves draw near,
is Fuji's lofty peak.
It thwarts the very clouds
     from their path.
Even the birds
   cannot reach its summit
     on their wings.
There, the snow drowns the flame
and the flame melts the snow.
I cannot speak of it,
I cannot name it,
this occultly dwelling god!
It envelops the waters
that we call a sea,
   the Sea of Se.
The river called Fuji
that men must cross
is but a stream of this mountain.
God who dwells there,
defender of the sun-source,
  the land of Yamato,
treasure of a mountain!
Though I gaze
on Fuji's lofty peak
    in Suruga,
I never tire.

320-321

Envoys

The fallen snow
on Fuji's peak
melts in the sixth month,
    on the fifteenth day,
only to fall again that night.[7]

Because of Fuji's lofty heights,
even the heavenly clouds,
        in their awe,
are thwarted from their path
and hang there trailing.

> The above poems are in the
> *Takahashi Mushimaro Collection.*
> Because of their resemblance to the
> other poems, they have been placed
> here.

322

*Poem by Yamabe Akahito upon reaching the hot springs
at Iyo*

    with tanka

Many are the lands
under the ancient sway
of the divine Princes,
    the Emperors,
but our Lord
finds Iyo good

---

[7] The Suruga *Fudōki* records the belief that the snow on Mount Fuji melted
on this date and began to fall again at midnight.

for its mountains and islands,
and stands on Izaniwa Hill
below the lofty peak
of its jagged, rockstrewn mountain,
and composes his songs there
and composes his words there.

As I gaze on the trees
clustered above the splendid springs,
I see the white fir that has grown
through the generation of men,
and hear the voices of the birds
that have not changed since ancient times.
Let it endure
 in its divinity
  to far ages in the future—
the place of our Lord's procession.

323

Envoy

I do not even know the year
when past courtiers
of the great palace
boarded their ships
 in Nikita harbor.

324

Poem by Yamabe Akahito when he climbed Kagu Hill

 with tanka

On Kamunabi Hill,
 shrine of the gods,
  in Mimoro,

the spruce is grown thick
with the five hundred branches
    it stretches forth.
Time and again,
  like the constant generations
      of the spruce,
and never ceasing,
  like the jewelled vine,
I would always pass
through Asuka's ancient capital.
There the mountains are lofty
and the river's flow is broad and grand.
Cranes soar wildly
through the morning clouds,
and frogs sing noisily
in the evening mist.
Each time I see it
I find myself in tears,
as my mind turns to the past.

325

Envoy

Like the rising mists
  that hold over the pools
    of the Asuka River,
this yearning does not pass.

326

*Poem by Prince Kadobe upon looking out from Naniwa
and seeing the light from the fishermen's lampfires*

Gazing out,
I see the points of fires
that fishermen have lit
    in Akashi Bay,
like the yearning for my wife
that has flared from me.

327

*Poem by the Priest Tsūkan when some girls wrapped up
a dried bonito and sent it to him, playfully praying for
his welfare*

Why, when I take this
out to the offing
and toss it in the ocean,
does it come back to life?

328

Poem by Ono Oyu, the Vice-Commander of the Dazaifu

The capital at Nara,
    beautiful in blue earth,
flourishes now
like the brilliant fragrance
of the flowers in bloom.

329 and 330

Two poems by Ōtomo Yotsuna, captain of the frontier guards at the Dazaifu

Among all the lands
under the sway of our Lord,
   who rules in peace,
my thoughts turn to the capital.

Now that the wisteria
are in full bloom,
sweeping down like waves,
do your thoughts, my Lord,
turn to the capital at Nara?

331-335

Five poems by Lord Ōtomo Tabito, Commander of the Dazaifu

331

Can I hope to regain
the full bloom of my youth,
or will I probably die
before I can ever see again
the capital at Nara?

332

Could my life
be granted permanence,
so that I could go again
to see the stream at Kisa
that I saw long ago?

333

Turning things over in my mind,
    mind like a field
        of shallow reeds,[8]
the memories return
of my old native village.

334

On my sleeve I pin the day lily—
    "grass of forgetfulness"—
so that somehow I may forget
my old village of Asuka
    by Kagu Hill.[9]

335

I trust my journey won't be long;
may Ime no Wada,
    the Abyss of Dreams,
not turn into rapids
but still be an unmoving pool.

---

[8] A pun links the "field" (*hara*) and the last two syllables of *tsubara*. The expression in the original, *tsubara tsubara ni mono omou*, is literally something like "to think of things intricately and turningly." But the pun seems to suggest an *image* for a mental act as well as the purely formal link by sound.

[9] The day lily is "*wasuregusa.*"

336

Poem by the Priest Mansei about floss-silk

> He was the imperial attendant who
> built the Kannonji Temple in
> Tsukushi. His lay name was Kasa
> Maro.

Keeping it with me,
I have yet to put it on.
But it looks warm,
this floss-silk from Tsukushi.

337

Poem by Yamanoue Okura, upon leaving a banquet

Okura shall take his leave now.
My child must be crying
and its mother,
who bears it on her back,
must be waiting for me.

338-350

*Thirteen poems in praise of wine by Lord Ōtomo
Tabito, the Commander of the Dazaifu*

338

Rather than engaging
in useless worries,
it's better to down a cup
of raw wine.

339

Great sages of the past
gave the name of "sage" to wine.
How well they spoke!

340

What the Seven Wise Men
    of ancient times
wanted, it seems,
        was wine.

341

Rather than making pronouncements
    with an air of wisdom,
it's better to down the wine
and sob drunken tears.

342

What is most noble,
  beyond all words
  and beyond all deeds,
is wine.

343

Rather than be half-heartedly human,
I wish I could be a jug of wine
and be soaked in it!

344

How ugly!
   those men who,
      with airs of wisdom,
         refuse to drink wine.
Take a good look,
and they resemble apes.

345

How could even
a priceless treasure
be better than a cup
     of raw wine?

346

How could even a gem
that glitters in the night
be as good as drinking wine
and cleansing the heart?

347

Here in this life,
on these roads of pleasure,
it is fun to sob drunken tears.

348

As long as I have fun
    in this life,
let me be an insect or a bird
    in the next.

349

Since all who live
must finally die,
let's have fun
while we're still alive.

350

Smug and silent airs of wisdom
are still not as good
as downing a cup of wine
and sobbing drunken tears.

351

Poem by the Priest Mansei

To what shall I compare
        this life?
the way a boat
    rowed out from the morning harbor
        leaves no traces on the sea.

352

Poem by Prince Akayue

The cranes are crying
among the reeds.
Your harbor winds
  must be blowing coldly,
        Cape Tsuo.

353

Poem by Shakutsūgan

The white clouds
    over Takaki Mountain
        in splendid Yoshino
are thwarted from their path,
and hang there trailing.

354

Poem by Heki Wo'oyu

When evening comes,
the smoke from the salt they burn
        by Nawa Cove
cannot get by,
and hangs trailing on the mountain.

355

Poem by Oishi Mahito

They say the gods dwelled there,
Ōnamuchi and Sukunahikona.
How many generations
have passed since then
in these caverns of Shitsu?

356

Poem by Kami Komaro

Today too
are they bright and clear,
those shallows of the Asuka River
where the frogs cry every evening?

357-362

Six poems by Yamabe Akahito

357

I see, behind Nawa Cove,
an island on the offing,
and from the boat
    they row around it
it looks like they are fishing.

358

Little boat
rowed around Muko Bay,
enviable little boat
watching Awa Island
 in the background
  as it goes by.

359

On the Abe Island rocks,
where the cormorants nest,
the waves pound,
 never letting up,
nor do, these days,
 my thoughts of Yamato.

360

When the tide ebbs,
cut the sleek seaweed
and store it.
If my wife at home
wants a souvenir from the beach,
what else can I give her?

361

You, my Lord,
must now be crossing Sanu Hill
 in the dawn,
  in the chilly autumn wind.
I wish I had lent you my cloak.

362

Like the gulfweed,
the "name-telling weed,"
that grows on the osprey-rooked
inlets in the rocky shore,
tell me your name—
even if your parents find out.

363

A variant has, for 362,

Like the gulfweed,
the "name-telling weed,"
that grows on the osprey-rooked
inlets in the rocky shore,
come now, tell me your name—
even if your parents find out.

364 and 365

*Two poems written by Kasa Kanamura at Shiotsu
Mountain*

Brave men, shoot,
the tips of your bows quivering!
May the one who later finds your arrow
recount it to the ages.

As I cross over Shiotsu Mountain,
my horse stumbles;
the ones at home
    must be longing for me.

366

*Poem by Kasa Kanamura as he boarded his ship in
Tsunoga Harbor*

with tanka

From Tsunoga Beach
on the Sea of Koshi,
we latched and lowered the cross-oars
    from our great ship,
and set into
    the whale-hunted sea lanes.
As we rowed forth,
    gasping for breath,
I saw, by Tayui Cove,
    Tayui
        of the brave men,
smoke from the salt
the fishergirls were burning.
But I was alone,
    on a journey,
        with grass for pillow,
and there was no point in looking.
So, like the strand of jewels
    the god of the ocean
    wraps around his wrist,
I wrapped my heart with memories
of the island, Yamato.

367

Envoy

Tayui Cove
on the sea of Koshi
captures the heart
of this journeyer,
and turns my thoughts
back to Yamato.

368

Poem by Lord Isonokami

We latch and lower
    the many cross-oars
        from our great ship
and, in awe of our Lord's command,
we row along the rocky bend.

> Present investigation shows that there
> was an Isonokami Koshimaro, who
> was appointed governor of Echizen.
> But was it this particular Lord
> Isonokami who wrote the above
> poem?

369

Poem in response

The men led by the minister
    of the warrior clans
sway to the will of our Lord.

> The name of the author of the above
> poem is yet unclear. However, it does
> appear in the *Kasa Kanamura
> Collection*.

370

Poem by Lord Abe Hironiwa

I have been waiting for you
with a dismal longing
like the dampness
of this overcast
but unraining evening.

371

*Poem by Prince Kadobe, Governor of Izumo, thinking of
the capital*

Plover on the river banks
where it flows into the Ou Sea,
when you cry
        so my heart
turns to the Saho River,
        my home.

372

*Poem by Yamabe Akahito when he climbed to the fields
of Kasuga*

    with tanka

Among the hills of Kasuga,
where the spring sun is dimmed,
on Mikasa Mountain,
    like the crown
        on a lofty altar,
the clouds trail every morning
and the halcyon's cry never ceases.
Like the distant clouds

my heart hesitates,
and like that bird
I weep my unrequited love.
Through the day,
    each day,
and through the night,
    each night,
I stand here
and I yearn
for the girl I cannot meet.

373

Envoy

On Mikasa Mountain,
    like the crown
        on a lofty altar,
the birds cease crying
only to start again—
such is my longing for her.

374

Poem by Isonokami Otomaro

Don't let anyone else
wear Kasa Mountain,
the "crown," the hat I'm saving
        in case it rains—
even if it means they get soaked!

375

Poem written by Prince Yuhara at Yoshino

In the pools of the Natsumi River
   in splendid Yoshino
the duck is crying—
there, in the mountains' shadow.

376 and 377

Two banquet poems by Prince Yuhara

In the inner depths of my heart,
like the depths of a jewelled box,
I think of her, with her sleeves swaying
fine as dragonfly wings.
See her, my Lords.

Though I see her always—
in the morning and the day—
like white clouds
  on blue mountain peaks,
she is ever precious, my Lords.

378

*Poem by Yamabe Akahito about the garden of the late
Prime Minister Fujiwara Fubito*

The years have deepened
on the ancient, crumbling embankment,
and waterweeds have spread
over the rims of the pond.

379

Poem of prayer by Lady Ōtomo Sakanoue

with tanka

O gods
who have been born to us
from the far fields of heaven,
I tie pure white strands of mulberry
to the branches of the sacred tree
   in the inland mountains,
I plant offering jars in the earth
and string many bamboo beads
down a trailing cord.
I am prostrate—
my knees are bent
like a wild boar's.
Wrapped in my woman's cloak,
in this state I implore you:
Can I not meet my man?

380

Envoy

Holding in my hands
a pile of mulberry strands,
in this state I implore you:
Can I not meet my man?

> The above poem was written when
> offerings were made to the gods of
> the Ōtomo clan, in winter, the
> eleventh month, of the fifth year of
> Tempyō (733). Therefore this is
> referred to as a poem of prayer.

381

Poem sent by the maiden of Tsukushi to a traveller

Don't let your heart
race with thoughts of home.
Watch the winds
with care before you go,
for the sea road is a savage one.

382

*Poem by Tajihi Kunihito upon climbing Tsukuba
Mountain*

Many are the lofty mountains
    in the eastern country,
    where the cock cries,
but since the age of the gods
men have told of Tsukuba Mountain,
the one beautiful to look upon
    with its noble peaks
    rising side by side—
        a pair of gods—
and climbed to the summit
    to view the land.
It is still shackled in winter's bonds,
    not yet time for climbing,
but if I passed by
without seeing its view,
it would make me yearn even more.
And so I have come,
struggling up the mountain path
through the melting snow.

383

Envoy

I could not merely glance
casually from afar
   at Tsukuba's peak,
but came up to the summit,
struggling up the path
through the melting snow.

384

Poem by Yamabe Akahito

The cockscomb I planted
and raised by my cottage
has withered.
Yet I think I shall not learn
    a lesson from it,
but sow its seeds again.

385-387

Three poems about the goddess of the mulberry branch[10]

Because hail-struck
   Kishimi Mountain
      is steep,
I let go of the grass I was picking
and take hold of my girl's hand.

   One source states that the above
   poem was given to the goddess of the

---

[10] In the legend, a mulberry branch floating down the Yoshino River is caught in a trap. A man named Umashine picks it from the trap, whereupon it turns into a woman. He takes her for his wife, but eventually she flies back to heaven.

mulberry branch by Umashine, a man
of Yoshino. However, this poem does
not appear in the legend of the
mulberry branch.

If a mulberry branch
comes down the stream this evening,
how could I not set a trap,
how could I not try to catch it?

If, in that ancient time,
there had been no man
to set a trap,
it would still be here—
that mulberry branch!

The above poem is by Wakamiya
Ayumaro.

388

A poem of travel

with tanka

Inscrutable are the ways of the sea,
casting up Awaji Island in its center
and sending the white waves cresting to Iyo.
When dusk falls
its tides swell
through Akashi's full-moon straits,
when dawn breaks
its tides recede through them.

In fear of the roaring waves,
we secluded our ship
on Awaji's rocky shore,

and have passed this night
    sleepless,
        wondering
when it would open into dawn,
and now the pheasants at Asano
    above the waterfall
have risen, and announce the morning
with their rustling.
Come lads, quick to the oars
    and let's be away!
The surface of the sea is calm.

389

Envoy

We have rowed along the island,
    round by Cape Minume,
and now the cranes flock and cry
as I long for Yamato.

> The above poems were recited by
> Wakamiya Ayumaro. But it is not yet
> clear who wrote them.

METAPHORICAL POEMS

390

Poem by Princess Ki

Even the duck
that circles round the bends
        of Karu Pond
never has to sleep alone
on the sleek seaweed.

391

*Poem by the Priest Mansei, the imperial attendant who
built the Kanzeonji Temple in Tsukushi*

Standing thick ends of branches in the earth
as offering to the mountain god,
they have chopped the trees
        on Ashigara Mountain,
chopped them as lumber for the ships—
a waste of such good wood!

392

*Poem on the plum blossom by Ōtomo Momoyo, captain
of the Dazaifu*

I forgot the plum blossom
on that pitch-black night.
I came away without picking it,
though I had meant to.

393

Poem about the moon by the Priest Mansei

Who would not want to see it,
though it is half-hidden?
Even from afar
I would view the moon
as it lingers on the mountain's edge.

394

Poem by Yo Myōgun

The little pine
on the beach at Suminoe
that I have decided on
and tied my marker to—
later it will still be mine.

395-397

Three poems sent to Ōtomo Yakamochi by Lady Kasa

I dyed my dress
with the violet grass
that grows on the fields of Tsukuma,
but before I could wear it
its colors were exposed.

Distant are the grassy plains of Mano
           in Michinoku;
men say you can conjure them
in your heart, and yet—

Strong-rooted, like the sedge
on the base of the rocks
    in the inland mountains,
are the feelings
we bound our hearts with—
I cannot forget.

398-399

Two poems on the plum blossom by Fujiwara Yatsuka

> Yatsuka's later name was Matate; he
> was the third son of Fusasaki.

When the plum tree
that blossoms by my woman's house
bears its fruit—
whenever that may be—
then let us decide.

When the flowering tree,
   the flowering plum tree,
that blossoms by my woman's house
bears its fruit,
I shall do with it as I desire.

400

Poem on the plum blossom by Ōtomo Surugamaro

Men say the plum flowers
blossom only to fall,
but not from the branch
I tie my marker to.

401

Poem recited by Lady Ōtomo Sakanoue at a feast of her relatives

Not knowing that the guardian
of the mountain was there,
I tied and raised my marker
    on that mountain—
tied it to my shame!

402

Poem written in immediate response by Ōtomo Surugamaro

Even if the guardian
of the mountain was there,
I doubt anyone would undo
the marker that my Lady tied.

403

Poem sent by Ōtomo Yakamochi to the daughter of the same Sakanoue house

How can I make sure it stays in my hand,
this gem I would constantly gaze on,
in the morning and throughout the day?

404

Poem by a maiden in response to one sent her by Saeki Akamaro

If only the shrine
  of the raging god
    were not there,
I would sow my millet
on the fields of Kasuga.

405

A further poem by Saeki Akamaro sent in response to hers

If your millet were sown
on the fields of Kasuga,
I would go there again and again,
following the grazing deer.
But the shrine stops me.

406

Another poem by the Lady in response

That is not the god I worship.
Brave man, you should attend
to the god who is with you.

407

Poem by Ōtomo Surugamaro when he wed the younger sister of the same Sakanoue house

You say the little leek you planted
in the village of Kasuga,
  where the spring is misted,
is still young and tender,
yet now it must be spreading its leaves.

408

Poem sent by Ōtomo Yakamochi to the elder sister of the same Sakanoue house

You should have been
a flower of the wild pink;
every morning I would pick you
    and take you in my hands,
and every day I would cherish you.

409

Poem by Ōtomo Surugamaro

Again and again I think of her—
  a thousand waves
    lapping my heart
      in a single day—
yet how hard it is to wrap that jewel
    around my wrist.

410

Poem about the orange tree by Lady Ōtomo Sakanoue

Now that I have given away
the orange tree that I planted
and raised in my garden,
I am distracted with regret—
I rise, I sit, I rise again—
but there is no use.

411

Poem in response

Since, my woman, you have planted
the orange tree in your garden
so close to me,
you cannot stop it
from bearing its fruit.

412

Poem by Prince Ishihara

I will sway this way and that
to the whims of your heart,
you who are to me
like the unique and precious jewel
nestled in a crown of hair.[11]

---

[11] The *Lotus Sutra* refers to "the single jewel on the crown of hair," and in Buddhism this is a metaphor for the highest enlightenment. In this poem the metaphysical symbol is used for a more secular appeal.

413

Poem recited at a banquet by Ōami Hitonushi

Too wide, the gaps between the threads
of this coarse wisteria cloth
the fishers of Suma are clad in
when they burn the salt;
I have yet to wear it to my comfort.

414

Poem by Ōtomo Yakamochi

The foothill-trailing mountain
is jagged with rocky cliffs,
and the hard-rooted sedge
     will not give,
so I will just tie my marker there and go.

LAMENTS

415

Poem by Prince Uenomiya Shōtoku, written in his grief when he found the body of a dead man on Tatsuta Mountain during his procession to Takaharanoi

> This was during the reign of Empress
> Suiko, who ruled the realm under
> heaven from the palace at Owarita
> (592-628).

If he were home
he would be pillowed
in his wife's arms,
but here on a journey
he lies with grass for pillow—
traveler, alas!

416

Poem by Prince Ōtsu, weeping on the banks of Iware Pond when he was about to be put to death

The duck that cries
in Iware Pond,
   where the vines
   crawl on the rocks:
will I see it just today,
and tomorrow be hidden in the clouds?

> The above incident occurred in
> winter, the tenth month, of the first
> year of Akamitori (686), during the
> period of the Fujiwara Palace.

BY THE AUTHOR

Hōryūji, the temple founded by Prince Shōtoku (poem III.415)

417-419

Three poems by Princess Tamochi written when Prince Kōchi was buried on Kagami Mountain in the land of Toyo

Did it suit my Prince's spirit well,
that he should choose Kagami Mountain,
       in the land of Toyo,
as his eternal shrine?

It seems he has raised a door of stone
before his tomb on Kagami Mountain,
       in the land of Toyo,
and concealed himself inside.
Though I wait for him, he will not come.

Oh that my arms had strength
to smash this door of stone!
But I am a weak-limbed woman,
I do not know what to do.

420

Poem by Princess Niu upon the death of Prince Iwata

    with tanka

"Our Prince, graceful
like the soft bamboo,
our red-cheeked Lord
is dead,"
spoke the messenger
with his jewelled catalpa staff,
"and enshrined as a god
in the mountains of Hatsuse,

the hidden land."
Are these lies I have heard?
Oh are these words of madness?
My regret swells between heaven and earth,
mine is the greatest regret in the world.
If only I had gone
to the ends of heaven and earth,
to the distant reaches
  of the heavenly clouds
(with or without my cane),
and divined him out with evening sorcery
and divined him out with sorcery of stones,[12]
and raised an altar in my house
and planted offering jars in the ground
            by my pillow
and strung bamboo beads down a trailing cord,
            leaving not a gap,
and hung strands of mulberry on my arms!
If only I had picked the seven-jointed sedge
from the fields of Sasara in Heaven
and, standing on the riverbanks
of the far firmament,
performed ablutions and prayed for him!
But now our Lord lies enshrined
above the cliffs
    of a towering mountain.

---

[12] In "evening sorcery," one stood at a fork in the road and divined things from the random words spoken by passersby. "Sorcery of stones" was a form of fortune-telling using the weights of different stones.

421 and 422

Envoys

Are these lies,
are these words of madness?
That you lie above the cliffs
of a towering mountain!

My thoughts of you
shall not easily pass
like the grove of cedars
on Furu Mountain in Isonokami.[13]

423

Poem by Prince Yamakuma in his grief upon the death
of this same Prince Iwata

The one who, every morning,
walked the road to Iware,
    where the vines
    crawl on the rocks,
thought as he passed by
that in the fifth month,
   when the cuckoo cries,
he would string the iris
and the orange blossoms
      like jewels
to decorate his hair,
and in the ninth month,
   in the season of the rains,
pick the scarlet leaves
for his garland,

[13] This poem is based on a pun linking "*sugi*," "cedars," and "*sugu*," "to
pass."

that thus he would go back and forth
    forever,
    like the jewelled vine,
    without end,
    to the distant future,
    for ten thousand ages,
never ceasing.
But now must I contemplate our Lord
    from a distant realm?

     One source states that the above
     poem is by Kakinomoto Hitomaro.

424 and 425

One book has the following two envoys,

The maiden of Hatsuse,
the hidden land,
had a bracelet wrapped around her wrist;
now do they not say
its string is cut,
its jewels scattered?

Though my Lord walks grieving
through Hatsuse,
where the river winds are cold,
can he even find someone
who resembles her?

     One source states that Prince
     Yamanaka wrote the above two
     poems in place of Prince Iwata
     following the death of Princess Ki.

426

*Poem written by Kakinomoto Hitomaro in his grief
when he saw a corpse on Kagu Hill*

Whose husband here
sought shelter on his journey,
        grass for pillow,
his homeland forgotten,
though his family waits there?

427

*Poem by Osakabe Tarimaro upon the death of Taguchi
Hiromaro*

If I offer prayers
to the god of this winding slope
    with eighty bends,
might I meet the one
who has passed beyond?

428

*Poem written by Kakinomoto Hitomaro when they
cremated the maiden of Hijikata in the mountains of
Hatsuse*

Wandering between the mountains
of Hatsuse, the hidden land,
can those clouds be the girl?

429 and 430

*Two poems written by Kakinomoto Hitomaro when, at
Yoshino, they cremated the maiden of Izumo, who had
died by drowning*

Not mist, yet from the mountain gap
she rises, the girl of Izumo,
and trails on the peaks of Yoshino.

The black hair
of the girl of Izumo,
where rise the eightfold clouds,
floats out over the depths
of the Yoshino River.

431

*Poem by Yamabe Akahito when he passed the grave of
the maiden of Mama in Kazushika*

with tanka[14]

I have heard her tomb is here,
the maiden of Mama in Kazushika
with whom the man
they say lived in the ancient past
undid his sash
        of Yamato-patterned cloth,
for whom he built a sleeping hut
and called her there to be his wife.
I have heard it is here,
but (is it for the black pines'
thick foliage

[14] A footnote after the phrase "with tanka" gives her name in the Eastern
dialect: "*Kazushika no Mama no tego* (rather than *otome*)."

or is it for time's passing long
and far away like the evergreen roots?)
I cannot find it.
Yet at least her story,
at least her name
I shall never forget.

432 and 433

Envoys

I too have seen it;
let me tell other men
of the place where her tomb is,
the maiden of Mama in Kazushika.

My thoughts turn to the maiden
who cut, they say,
the sleek swaying seaweed
in Mama Cove in Kazushika.

434-437

*In the fourth year of Wadō (711), Kawabe Miyahito
found the corpse of a beautiful woman in the field of
pines at Himeshima, and wrote these four poems in his
grief*

Though I see the white azaleas
by Miho Inlet,
     where the winds are quick,
I am lonely, for I think
of the one who is gone.

How I regret the withering
of the grasses on the rocky shore

that must have felt the hands
of the youth of majestic Kume.

These days, when the gossip
        flies so thick,
if you were a jewel
I would wrap you round my wrist,
and cease my painful longing.

My heart and yours are pure,
like the banks of Kiyomi River,
      "the crystal stream,"
so let us not have thoughts
      we might regret.

> Present consideration shows that the
> above poems share the same title as
> that of II. 228-229 in the year of
> composition, the place, the girl's
> corpse and the poet's name.
> However, the words in the poem are
> different, and it is impossible to
> distinguish the sets of poems one way
> or the other. Therefore, we have
> placed this additional set here at a
> later place in the collection.

438-440

*Three poems from the fifth year of Jinki (728) by Lord
Ōtomo Tabito, Commander of the Dazaifu,
remembering a dead woman*

Will I find another
to take my arms
for her finely woven pillow
as my beloved took them?

The time has come
when I must return.
Whose arms will pillow me
   in the capital?

When I sleep alone
in my desolate house
  in the capital,
it will be more painful
than the lonely sleep of a journey.

441

*Poem by Princess Kurahashibe in the sixth year of Jinki
(729), after Prince Nagaya, the Minister of the Left, was
put to death*[15]

Though it is not yet time
for your enshrinement in a tomb,
in awe of our Lord's command
you hide yourself in the clouds.

442

A poem sorrowing over Prince Kashiwadebe

See, that life's an empty thing:
this gleaming moon
    has waxed and waned.

  The name of the author of the above
  poem is yet unclear.

---

[15] Prince Nagaya was accused of plotting to overthrow the government,
and was forced to commit suicide, along with his wife and four sons. The
incident may have been contrived by the powerful Fujiwara clan as a way to
remove Nagaya as a possible rival.

443

*Poem by the sub-official Ōtomo Minaka in the first year
of Tempyō (729), when Hasetsukabe Tatsumaro, a
scribe from the land of Settsu in the Office of Land
Distribution, strangled himself*

with tanka

"A warrior
who comes to serve
from lands that lie
at the distant reaches
   of the heavenly clouds
must stand guard
outside the godly palace
      of the Emperors
and attend his Lord
inside those precincts,
thus passing down the name
   of his ancestors
to distant ages in the future,
far and long as the jewelled vine."

Since the day he departed
with these words
     to his father and mother,
     to his wife and children,
his mother,
     with her milk-full breasts,
planting offering jars
in the ground before her,
holding mulberry strands in one hand
and delivering up
     soft prayer cloth in the other,
begged the gods

of heaven and earth
that her son be granted peace,
that his life be sound.

But while she waited,
rising, sitting, rising again
            with worry,
wondering how many years,
how many months and days
until her son,
flourishing in splendor
like the azaleas in fragrant bloom,
would, like the blackbird,
crossing rivers and seas,
return,
        he, in his awe
of our Lord's command,
served from dawn til dusk,
    without even a moment
    to dry his white cloth robes,
in the land of Naniwa,
where sunlight sweeps across the bay,
until the years passed away
like a strand of rough gems.
And now—what could have been
in his mind?—
it seems he has left behind
this precious world
as dew or frost
are left on the ground—
though it was not his time.

444 and 445

Envoys

Yesterday you were alive,
but now—how strange—
you trail like the clouds
over pines on the beach.

You who departed, without even leaving
words for your messenger,
        with his jewelled catalpa staff,
to take to your wife who waits,
wondering when you will return!

446-450

*Five poems by Lord Ōtomo Tabito, Commander of the
Dazaifu, written in winter, the twelfth month, of the
second year of Tempyō (730), when he set out on the
road for the capital*

446

The juniper at Tomo Cove
lasts eternally,
but my wife,
    who gazed on it,
            is gone.

447

Each time I gaze on the juniper
by the rocky shore at Tomo Cove,
I cannot forget my wife,
who gazed on it with me.

448

If I ask the juniper,
whose roots crawl
        over the rocky shore,
where is the one who gazed on it,
will it tell me?

> The above three poems were written
> the day he passed Tomo Cove.

449

Returning past Cape Minume,
where I came with my wife,
and gazing out alone,
my eyes are filled with tears.

450

Passing this cape alone,
that we two gazed on together
when we went the other way,
my heart is saddened.

> The above two poems were written
> the day he passed Cape Minume.

451-453

*Three poems upon returning to the home in one's native
village*

This empty house,
with no one here,
is more painful to be in

than to be on a lonely sojourn,
    with grass for pillow.

How tall the trees,
and thick their foliage,
in the garden
that my wife and I built together.

Each time I see
the plum tree
that my wife planted,
my heart is choked
and tears stream from my eyes.

454-459

*Six poems written when the Chancellor, Lord Ōtomo
Tabito, died, in autumn, the seventh month, of the third
year of Tempyō (731)*

454

Beloved Lord who flourished!
If you were here
you would beckon me to serve you
today and tomorrow.

455

It was destined
to come but to this,
and yet, my Lord, you asked me
if the bush clover are in bloom!

456

Longing for you,
there is nothing I can do,
so, like the cranes
    among the reeds,
I weep and cry aloud
in the morning and the evening.

457

Lord whom I thought I would serve
far into the distant future,
you are no more,
and my heart has lost its bearing.

458

Crawling like a baby,
I weep, and I cry aloud
in the morning and the evening,
now that you, my Lord, are gone.

> The above five poems were written
> by Tabito's servant, Yo Myōgun,
> who loved his master as a dog or
> horse would, unable to repress the
> emotions in his heart.

459

My Lord, I never tired
   to look upon you
   while you were alive;
such sadness now that you are gone
like the scattered leaves of autumn.

> Agatanoinukai Hitogami,
> Administrator of the Board of Inner
> Ceremonies, was ordered to minister
> to Lord Ōtomo's illness. But the
> medicine had no effect. Running
> water cannot be stopped—the Lord
> died. Agatanoinukai, grief-struck over
> this, wrote the above poem.

460

*Poem by Lady Ōtomo Sakanoue in the seventh year of
Tempyō (735), grieving over the death of the nun
Rigwan*

   with tanka

Hearing that this
      is a good land,
she came from Silla,
land of mulberry-woven nets,
and crossed to Japan,
where she had no relations,
no brothers and sisters to talk to.
The sun-blessed capital
of our Lord's realms
is packed with many quarters and houses,
but—what could have been
in her mind?—

she was drawn,
   like a weeping child
      to its parents,
to the Saho mountainside,
so foreign to her.
There she built a house
   where she could place
   her well-woven pillow,
and has dwelled there
through the long years.
But she could not escape
the fact that all who live
         must die;
while everyone she depended on
was away on a journey,
   with grass for pillows,
she crossed the Saho River
     in the morning
and, glancing back
on the fields of Kasuga,
disappeared toward the mountainside
as one fades
into the gathering darkness of evening.
There is nothing I can say,
     nothing I can do,
so I wander
      all alone
without a moment
to dry my white mourning robes—
do these tears
I cry in my grief
trail as clouds over Arima Mountain
and fall as rain?

461

Envoy

Life's course cannot be stopped,
and so she is gone
out from the house
where she kept her well-woven pillow,
and is hidden in the clouds.

> The above refer to a nun from Silla
> in Korea, her name Rigwan. She felt
> our ruler's virtue from afar, and came
> to our holy realm and was
> naturalized. She lived in the home of
> Lord Ōtomo Yasumaro, Chancellor
> and Commander of the Army, and
> had been there for some years when,
> in the seventh year of Tempyō (735),
> she suddenly came down with a fatal
> disease, and was soon away to the
> realm of the dead. At this time Lady
> Ishikawa was at the hot springs of
> Arima for her cure, and was unable
> to attend the funeral. Her daughter,
> however, asked that she be allowed
> to interrupt her journey and go alone
> to perform the obsequies. Thus she
> wrote this poem and sent it to her
> mother at the hot springs.

462

*Poem written by Ōtomo Yakamochi in summer, the
sixth month, of the eleventh year of Tempyō (739), in
his grief over his dead concubine*

Soon the autumn winds
will be blowing coldly;
how can I sleep
through the long nights alone?

463

Poem in response by his brother, Ōtomo Fumimochi

"Am I to sleep," you ask,
"through the long nights alone?"
Such words will stir memories
of the one who is gone.

464

Another poem by Yakamochi, written as he gazed on the
wild pink in blossom by the paving stones

The pink in the garden
that my wife planted
for me to admire
when autumn comes—
now it has bloomed.

465

Poem by Yakamochi in the next month, grieving over
the autumn wind

Though I know
the world of the living
is not eternal,
yet how the cold autumn wind
makes me remember her!

466

Another poem by Yakamochi

    with tanka

The flowers have bloomed
       in my garden.
But though I look on them
my heart is unfulfilled.
If my beloved wife were here
we would stand side by side
  like the splendid ducks,
and pick these blossoms
and show them to each other.
But hers was the transitory
fate of the living,
and so, fading like mist or frost,
she disappeared,
   like the setting sun,
toward the foothill-trailing
        mountain path.
It racks my breast to think of it.
I cannot express it in words,
I cannot give it a name—
here in the realm
of life's traceless passing,
there is nothing I can do.

467-469

Envoys

No matter when her time came,
she would have departed
with pain in her heart,
           my wife
who left her infant behind.

If I had known the path
by which she left this world,
I would have placed a barrier there
to hold her back.

In the garden
she used to look upon
the flowers have bloomed;
time has passed,
though the tears I weep
have yet to dry.

470-474

*Five more poems Yakamochi wrote, his grief yet
unstilled*

470

Though it is destined
to come but to this,
my wife and I trusted in life
as if it would last
           a thousand years.

471

My wife departed from our home.
I could not hold her back
so I have hidden her
    in the mountain,
and my heart has lost its bearing.

472

Though my mind knows
that life never comes
        but to this,
how I cannot bear
these painful feelings!

473

Each time I see the mist
trailing on Saho Mountain,
I remember my wife—
        there is no day
when I do not weep.

474

In the past
I glanced at it casually,
but now that I realize
my wife's grave is there,
how beloved is Saho Mountain.

475-480

Six poems by Ōtomo Yakamochi, servingman to Prince Asaka, when the Prince passed away in spring, the second month, of the sixteenth year of Tempyō (744)

475

I hesitate to put it in words,
it is an awesome thing to speak.
Spring has come,
   with swaying branches,
       to the capital,
where I had hoped
that our Lord,
   divine Prince,
would rule the great land of Yamato
for ten thousand generations.
Now that the blossoms
spread over the mountainsides
and the young sweetfish
run in the river shallows,
in this season of daily-
growing brilliance,
are these lies I hear?
Are these words of madness?
His servingmen
have donned white mourning robes
and have carried his palanquin
up Wazuka Mountain,
and he has ascended
to rule the far heavens.
I collapse,
I weep,
splattered with mud,
but there is nothing I can do.

476 and 477

Envoys

I did not imagine
that our Lord is gone
to rule the heavens,
so I have glanced
with a neglecting look
at forested Wazuka Mountain.

Like flowers that blossom
to swathe the mountain
in a brilliant light,
but only to fall and scatter—
such was our Lord.

> The above three poems were written
> on the third day of the second
> month.

478

I hesitate to put it in words.
Our Lord,
          divine Prince,
summoned his many retainers
and led them out.
On his morning hunt
he drove the deer and boar
          from their lairs,
on his evening hunt
he drove the quail and pheasant
          from their lairs.
Pulling in the reins
of his royal steed,

he stopped and gazed out
        on Ikuji Mountain
to refresh his heart.
Now the flowers that bloomed
there among the thick foliage
have fallen away;
        such, it seems,
is the way of the world.
We trusted in our Lord
as, stirring his
        warrior's heart
and girding his waist
        with his swords,
he took his catalpa bow and quiver
and strapped them to his back.
We trusted that he
would always be thus
forever far and long
as heaven and earth,
for ten thousand generations.
But now in his palace
the servingmen cry and clamor
        like summer flies,
and clad themselves
in white mourning robes.
Their laughs and their merriness
fade from day to day.
I look, and I am saddened.

479 and 480

Envoys

The Ikuji Road
that our divine Prince—
how we loved him!—
passed and gazed on always
now lies waste.

Strapping the quiver,
famed with the Ōtomo name,
        to my back,
I served my Lord, trusting
it would be for ten thousand generations.
Now where can I place my heart?

481

Poem by Lord Takahashi, grieving over his dead wife

    with tanka

My wife and I vowed
to live together
        into new ages,
our bonds unbreakable
like a cord of jewels,
until our black hair
(side by side when we slept,
crossing our white sleeves
and swaying to each other)
turned white.
Our vows unfulfilled,
our desires unrealized,
she has left my white-sleeved arms

and departed from the house
    of her peaceful life,
leaving our crying child.
She has passed
beyond the edge
    of Sagara Mountain
        in Yamashiro,
fading like the morning mist.
There is nothing I can say,
        nothing I can do.
In the mornings I go out
from the marriage hut
where we slept together,
            and remember.
In the evenings
I go inside
        and grieve.
Each time our child
cries in my arms
I, though a man,
bear it on my back
and hold it close to me.
Weeping and crying aloud
like the morning birds,
I long for her,
but there is no use.
Though it is a thing
that cannot speak,
I find myself drawn
to the mountain
where my wife has gone inside.

482 and 483

Envoys

A matter of life's transience:
the mountain
I used to glance at casually
now is precious to me.

I shall go on weeping
and crying aloud
like the morning birds,
for there is no way for me
to meet my wife again.

> The above three poems were written
> by Lord Takahashi on the twentieth
> day of the seventh month. His
> personal name is yet unclear, but it is
> said he was the son of the imperial
> dinner steward.

BOOK FOUR

BY ISHIKAWA TADAYUKI

Nara: beneath the hills of Kasuga

Among the hills of Kasuga,
where the spring sun is dimmed,
on Mikasa Mountain,
   like the crown
     on a lofty altar,
the clouds trail every morning
and the halcyon's cry never ceases . . .

    Yamabe Akahito (from "Poem when he climbed to the
    fields of Kasuga," III.372)

PERSONAL EXCHANGES

484

*Poem sent by the wife of Emperor Nintoku to her
brother in Yamato*

Anyone could easily wait
          a day,
but having to wait
through these long days
is more than one can bear.

485

*Poem by the Sovereign who ruled the realm under
heaven from the Okamoto Palace*

    with tanka

Generation upon generation
have been born
since the time of the gods,
and men fill the land with their numbers,
going this way and that
like a flock of rustling ducks.
But you, whom I long for,
are not among them.
And so, through the day
    till it draws into dusk,
and so, through the night,
    till it brightens with dawn,
I long for you,

and stir through the nights
unable to sleep my sleep—
through these long nights.

486-487

Envoys

Though men pass by
like a flock of ducks
rustling over the mountain's edge,
still I am lonely—
for you are not among them.

Shall I spend these days in longing,
uncertain, like the Isaya River—
          "the unknowing"—
that flows by Toko Mountain
     on the road to Ōmi?

> Present consideration shows there
> were two "Okamoto Palaces," the
> Okamoto Palace at Takechi, where
> reigned Emperor Jomei, and the Later
> Okamoto Palace, where reigned
> Empress Saimei—two different ages,
> two different sovereigns. It is yet
> unclear which "Sovereign of the
> Okamoto Palace" is being referred to
> above.[1]

[1] Because the poem is addressed to a man, Empress Saimei is generally preferred by modern commentators. However, there are not a few same-sex personal exchanges with a similarity of conception and language to this one, suggesting that, lacking other evidence, the original annotation should be respected as is.

488

Poem by Princess Nukada, thinking of Emperor Tenji

Waiting for you, my Lord,
I sit here longing;
and the autumn wind blows,
fluttering the bamboo blinds
on the door to my house.

489

Poem by Princess Kagami

I envy you, who have
at least the wind to long for;
if I could wait, hoping
even the wind would come,
wherefore would I grieve?

490 and 491

Two poems by Fuki Toji

Is it because my thoughts of her
follow one upon another—
like the bridge of planks
across the shallows of Mano Cove—
that I see my wife in my dreams?

Come to me, my man,
    always, always,
like flowers of the lush weed
trailing over the river.
Could the season ever be wrong?[2]

---

[2] The words "lush weed" and "always" are both "*itsu mo.*"

492-495

Four poems by Tabe Ichihiko when he was sent to a post at the Dazaifu

492

What do you mean to do,
leaving me behind
whose longing for you
is greater than a weeping child's,
clutching his parent's sleeves?

493

When I go away, leaving her behind,
my wife will long for me,
spreading her black hair,
like a well-woven blanket,
                    over her bed—
through these long nights.

494

As my longing grows,
it is hatred I feel
for the one who introduced me
                    to my girl.

495

Like the faint moon
lingering on the mountain's edge
where the rising sun shimmers,

my Lord, I never tired of you
but now I must leave you behind
    the mountains that I cross.

496-499

Four poems by Kakinomoto Hitomaro

496

Though my heart
is a hundredfold in longing,
like the beach crinum
on fine Kumano's cove,
yet I cannot meet you face to face.

497

Were men of ancient times
like me,
    longing for their girls,
unable to sleep?

498

It is not only a thing of the present.
Men of ancient times,
longing even more than us,
cried out in their weeping.

499

Is it because
I would have him come
          a hundred times
that I do not tire
to gaze on your messenger?

500

*Poem by the wife of Go Dan'ochi, who stayed behind
when he went to the land of Ise*

Breaking off twigs of bush clover
          on the beach at Ise,
               of the divine wind,
you spread them
          for your sojourner's bed,
there on the rocky strand.

501-503

Three poems by Kakinomoto Hitomaro

501

I, who have thought of you
for as long as the fence of trees
has stood on ancient Furu Mountain,
where the maidens wave their sleeves!

502

How could I forget
              my wife's love
for as little as the inches
between the deer's antlers
as he walks across the summer fields?

503

Sombered, as the rustling died away
            from our silken clothes,
come away without a word
to my wife, who waits at home—
now I cannot bear the thought.

504

Poem by the wife of Kakinomoto Hitomaro

I shall not forget
the road to your house
on Sumi Hill—there
where I settled in with you—
as long as my life is spared.

505 and 506

Two poems by Lady Abe

What need for worries anymore?
Swaying,
my heart has drawn
to you, my Lord.

Do not worry over things, my man.
Whatever may come—
    be it fire or be it flood—
I will never be from your side.

507

Poem by the courtmaiden of Suruga

I slept afloat
on tears that streamed
from my well-woven pillow—
so intense was my longing.

508

Poem by Mikata Sami

From this evening,
when our sleeves draw apart,
my woman and I
will long painfully for each other—
there is no way for us to meet again.

509

*Poem by Tajihi Kasamaro when he went down to the
land of Tsukushi*

    with tanka

I stand by Mitsu Cove,
        that gleams like the mirror
        atop a courtwoman's box of combs,

and long for my wife,
    never undoing
        the red-hued sash
            she tied for me,
and, like the crying cranes
hidden in the morning mist
when darkness yields to dawn,
I weep and cry aloud.
Hoping to find solace
for a thousandth
of my thousand-folded longing,
I stand and gaze
in the direction of our home,
and see it is hidden
    in the white clouds
        trailing over Kazuraki Mountain,
        whose peaks range like blue banners.

I set out
    for barbarian frontiers
at the far reach of the heavens,
passing Awaji Island
directly before me
and glancing back
at Awashima behind.
Among pitched cries of sailors
        in the morning calm
and the splash of oars
        in the evening calm,
we have pushed through the waves
and veered between the reefs,
we have passed the rocky bend
        at Inabitsuma

and come across the seas
                        like water fowl.
And now, at Ie Island,
swaying lush on the rugged shore,
the *nanoriso* grass,
        the "name-telling":
O why have I come away
without telling my wife?

510

Envoy

I should have counted
the months and days till I return,
as she and I untied
each other's white-cloth sleeves—
and then come away.

511

*Poem by the wife of Lord Tagima Maro when he went
with the imperial procession to the land of Ise*

Where does my husband go?
Today is he crossing
Nabari Mountain
hidden in a deep
                inland place?[3]

---

[3] This is an exact repetition of poem no. 43.

512

Poem by Kaya, maiden of the thatch[4]

If we drew together
like harvesters where they cut
    on autumn fields,
    the fields ripe with grain,
would that give men cause
    to gossip of me?

513

Poem by Prince Shiki

I have wondered when
I could see you, woman—
    like the hallowed copse
    of little trees at Ohara.
And tonight we meet![5]

514

Poem by the Abe maiden

How I sewed
each and every seam
of that robe, my man,
    you wear,
and stitched in my emotion!

---

[4] Kaya seems to be the name of one of Emperor Jomei's concubines, "the maiden Kaya" (蚊屋娘), rewritten 草 ("grass" or "thatch") in a joking reference to the contents of the poem itself.

[5] This poem seems to be constituted by both a pun on the word "*itsu*" (meaning both "hallowed" and "when") and an association of the poet's difficulty in seeing his woman with the image of the copse itself, which often demarcates the sanctified precincts of a Shintō shrine.

515

Poem sent to the Abe maiden by Nakatomi Azumabito

As I sleep alone
the waistcord you tied for me
has come undone—
                    ill omen!
In my helplessness
I weep and cry aloud.

516

Poem by Lady Abe in response

I should have fastened it
with a triple-threaded string.
Now,
        now I regret it!

517

*Poem by Lord Ōtomo Yasumaro, Chancellor and
Commander General*

Though my hands
may even touch the sacred tree,
must I never touch you,
just because you are another's wife?

518

Poem by Lady Ishikawa

        of the great Ōtomo house at Saho

These days I do not see you,
who once came to me

fearlessly treading
the rough path along the mountains
by the fields of Kasuga.

519

Poem by Lady Ōtomo

> She was the mother of Prince Imaki.
> The Prince later was bestowed the
> surname Ōhara no Mahito.

You who always shut yourself in,
with the rain for your excuse:
was the rain that fell
  from the distant skies
when you came to me last night
  a lesson to you?

520

Poem added by someone[6] later in response

Will the rains not fall for me
  from the distant skies?
I could be shut inside
and spend the entire day
  with you, my Lord.

[6] Perhaps Ōtomo Yakamochi?

521

*Poem sent by the maiden of Hitachi to Lord Fujiwara
Umakai upon his return to service in the capital*

Do not forget, my Lord,
this eastern woman
who stands in the garden
    cutting and drying the hemp
    and bleaching the cloth.

522-524

*Three poems sent to Lady Ōtomo by Lord Fujiwara,
Civil Administrator of the capital*

522

Have I too become
wizened and antiqued,
  like the splendid old combs
  in the maidens' jewelled boxes—
unable to meet my woman?

523

They say a strong and patient man
    will wait a year,
but before I know it
I have fallen into longing again.

524

Though I lie beneath the softness
                of warm quilts,
I sleep not with my wife,
and how my skin is cold!

525-528

Four poems by Lady Ōtomo in response

525

Would that,
even a single night a year,
your pitch-black steed would come,
        treading over the pebbles
        in the Saho River.

526

Never do the ripples cease
in the shallows of the Saho River,
            where the plover cries,
nor does my longing for you.

527

Since there are times you do not come
even when you tell me you will come,
I cannot wait for you to come
when you say you probably will not come—
and you do say you probably will not come.

528

Wide are the shallows
at the Saho River crossing,
    where the plover cries,
and I would build a bridge of planks there
if I thought you were coming.

> The Lady who wrote the above was
> the daughter of the Saho Chancellor,
> Lord Ōtomo Yasumaro. She first wed
> Prince Hozumi, of the First Rank,
> and was cherished by him above all
> others. After the Prince's death this
> Lady was wed by Lord Fujiwara
> Maro. She lived in the village of
> Sakanoue, and therefore was named
> Lady Sakanoue.

529

Another poem by Lady Ōtomo Sakanoue

Do not cut the brushwood
on the heights
over the Saho River.
Let it be—
when spring comes a place
to hide and make love.

530

Poem sent by the Emperor to Princess Unakami

> Emperor Shōmu, who ruled the realm
> under heaven from the Nara Palace

I have no doubts
about my woman's love.
She is bound to me as tightly

as the stakes in the corral fence
that the red steed leaps.

> On present consideration, the above
> poem is a work imitating the ancient
> style. Perhaps he bestowed it to her
> on an appropriate occasion.[7]

531

Poem by Princess Unakami in response

> She was the daughter of Prince Shiki

How good to hear of your procession,
even the distant echo,
            the nightsound
                    of catalpa bowstrings
                    plucked on fingertips.

532 and 533

Two poems by Ōtomo Sukunamaro

> He was the third son of the Saho
> Chancellor, Ōtomo Yasumaro

Precious to me my daughter
      who goes away to serve
      at the sun-blessed palace:
to hold her back would be painful,
to give her up
will leave me helpless with despair.

---

[7] Nakanishi Susumu suggests an "appropriate occasion" would most likely
be a poetry gathering in which the participants were required to compose in
an ancient style.

How I envy the others
who can look upon my child
    until it wearies them:
as ebbtide's remnant waters
    gather in countless pools
    all over Naniwa Lagoon.

534

Poem by Prince Aki

    with tanka

Far away my wife—
she is not here with me
and the road to her,
    like a jewelled spear,
        is a long one.
And so each thought
    fills me with unease
and each sigh
    fills me with pain.
Oh to be a cloud
coursing through the splendid skies,
to be a high-soaring bird!
I would fly to her tomorrow
and speak to her—
for my sake,
    to know she is safe,
for her sake,
    to know I am safe.
Oh to be beside her now
as when we met before!

535

Envoy

We have let time stretch between us
since we pillowed each other in our arms,
    in our softly-woven sleeves;
a year has passed,
as I realize we no longer meet.

> Prince Aki exchanged vows with the
> courtmaiden of Yakami from the
> province of Inaba, longing for her
> with great intensity, his love at its
> highest peak. But her behavior made
> her guilty, by imperial judgement, of
> disrespect for the throne, and she was
> sent back to her home province.
> Upon this the Prince, his heart full of
> sorrow and lament, composed the
> above poems.

536

A poem of longing by Prince Kadobe

Will I walk the distant road
with unrequited longing,
like the dry lagoon
    where the tide has ebbed
        in the Ou Sea?[8]

> When Prince Kadobe was appointed
> governor of Izumo, he exchanged
> vows with a maiden in his
> jurisdiction. Before much time had
> passed, he ceased his visits to her. But
> after several months he found himself

---

[8] The poem is constituted by a pun linking *kata*, "lagoon," and *katamoi*, "unrequited longing."

in love with her again. He then
composed the above poem, and sent
it to the maiden.

537-542

Six poems sent to Prince Imaki by Princess Takata

537

Do not speak to me
with all your pretty words.
Being without you
for a single day, my Lord,
is more than I can bear.

538

Only because the gossip is so thick,
                their words so painful,
have I not met you.
Do not think, O my man,
that my heart has changed.

539

If only, my man,
you let me know you love me,
I would go out from my house
                to meet you,
however thick the gossip may be.

540

Was it because I feared
perhaps I would not see you,
          my man, again,
that I was helpless with despair
when we parted this morning?

541

Thick is the gossip
          in this world.
Let us meet, my man,
in the world to come—
even if not right away.

542

You never failed to come to me
but now, my Lord,
that your messenger does not appear,
it seems your heart sways
and hesitates to meet me.

543

*A poem requested by a maiden, for her to send to one of
the retainers who accompanied the imperial procession
to the land of Ki, in winter, the tenth month, of the first
year of Jinki (724)*

    Composed by Kasa Kanamura

My beloved husband
has gone with the many retainers
following our Sovereign

in his procession.
Setting out from the Karu Road[9]
with his eyes on Unebi Mountain,
    where the maidens
        wear strands of jewels,
he has entered onto the road to Ki,
    fine in hempen cloth.
My Lord must now be crossing
      Matsuchi Mountain,
gazing at the yellow leaves
that scatter and fly about,
and dimly I realize
he thinks not of me,
who loved him intimately,
but thinks instead how fine
is his grass-for-pillow journey!
Yet I cannot remain here,
    sitting still.
A thousand times I long
to follow my man in his trail,
but I am a weak-limbed woman
and when the guardians of the roads
    question me,
I would not know
what answer to give.
And so I rise to leave,
but stand here hesitating.

544 and 545

Envoys

**Rather than be left behind
    longing for you,**

[9] See Book Two, note 5.

would that I could be
        Imo and Se Mountains—
        "husband and wife"—
there in the land of Ki.

If I followed my man,
tracing his footsteps,
would the guardian
of the Ki barrier stop me?

546

*Poem composed when he won a maiden during the
imperial procession to the detached palace at
Mikanohara, in spring, the third month, of the second
year of Jinki (725)*

    By Kasa Kanamura

I only saw her in the distance,
        like the heavenly clouds,
where the roads,
        like jade spears,
                cross,
during my sojourn
at Mikanohara.
There was no way
        to speak with her,
so my desires
lay choked inside my heart.
But now the gods
        of heaven and earth
have disposed to let me cross
my well-woven sleeves with hers
and depend on her

as if she were my very own wife
               tonight—
would that this night
were long as a hundred autumn nights!

547 and 548

Envoys

Since that moment
when I saw her in the distance,
      like the heavenly clouds,
my heart, and my very being
have drawn to this girl!

Quickly this night has broken,
and the dawn
finds me in helpless despair.
How I prayed it would last
long as a hundred autumn nights!

549-551

*Three banqueting poems composed at the Ashiki horse
station in the land of Chikuzen, when Ishikawa Tarihito,
Deputy Vice-Commander of the Dazaifu, stopped there
on his return to the capital in the fifth year of Jinki (728)*

549

Gods of heaven and earth assist you
               till you reach your home,
my Lord who journeys
               with grass for pillow.

550

You are gone, my Lord,
whom I trusted in
as I would in a great ship,
and I shall long for you
until I see you face to face again.

551

Like the waves that draw
to the rocky bends of islands
    on the way to Yamato,
so without interval
    is my longing for you.

> The names of the authors of the
> above poems are yet unclear.

552

Poem by Ōtomo Miyori

Is it because, my Lord,
you wish me to die
that you go two ways,
on nights when you meet me
and nights when you do not?

553 and 554

Two poems sent to Lord Ōtomo Tabito, Commander of
the Dazaifu, by Princess Niu

You are far away
    as the distant reaches
        of the heavenly clouds.
Does my heart soar to you
and make me yearn like this?

Men of ancient times
raised the wine of Kibi to their lips.
But I am ill,
    and it does me no good.
Give me, instead, a screen
of bamboo treliss from your domain.

555

Poem sent by Lord Ōtomo Tabito, Commander of the
Dazaifu, to his Vice-Commander, Lord Tajihi
Agatamori, upon his return to the capital to become
Minister of Civil Affairs

The wine I have prepared
    to greet you with—
must I drink it
on the fields of Yasu
alone,
    with no companion?

556

Poem sent to Ōtomo Miyori by Princess Kamo

> She was the daughter of the late
> Prince Nagaya, Minister of the Left

Your ship from Tsukushi
       has yet to arrive,
but already I feel the sorrow
of seeing you, my Lord,
who treat me roughly.

557 and 558

*Two poems by Hashi Mimichi, composed while on the
sea lanes on his way up to the capital from Tsukushi*

Speed the great ship's oars!
And if we crash upon the rocks and keel,
       then let us keel—
if for my woman's sake.

I shall take back the prayer cloth
I hung on the shrine
       of the raging god,
for I have not met my woman.

559-562

*Four poems of longing by Ōtomo Momoyo,
Captain of the Dazaifu*

559

Having come through life
free of misfortune,
that I should fall into such longing
now that I am old!

560

What good will it do me
after I am dead from longing?
It is for the days I am alive
that I want to see my woman.

561

If you tell me you love me
when you do not love me,
the god of the Mikasa Shrine
        at Ono
will surely find you out.

562

That woman! She makes men
scratch their eyebrows without rest
in hopes that they may meet her—
        but in vain.[10]

---

[10] Popular superstition held that by scratching one's eyebrows one could
meet one's lover.

563 and 564

Two poems by Lady Ōtomo Sakanoue

Never until now
in this old life,
    when white hairs twine
    among the black,
have I fallen into longing like this.

Like the mountain sedge,
we have born no fruit between us,
yet they draw me to you
    in their gossip;
with whom, I wonder,
are you sleeping?

565

Poem by Princess Kamo

Like Ōtomo's noble cove,
I shall tell no one
that I have seen you,[11]
though we met face to face
    in the night
    when the moon shone crimson.

[11] The poem is based on a pun on the word *mitsu*, meaning both "noble cove" and the past tense of the verb "to see."

566 and 567

Two poems sent by Ōtomo Momoyo,
Captain of the Dazaifu, and another,
by express messenger

Cherishing you who journey,
    with grass for pillow,
I have come to be beside you,
come along the beach at Shika.

> The above poem is by Ōtomo
> Momoyo.

The day you cross Iwakuni Mountain
            in Suwa,
be sure to tie a prayer cloth
    to the gods of the pass,
for that road is a savage one.

> The above poem is by the Deputy Scribe
> Yamaguchi Wakamaro

> In the sixth month of the second year of
> Tempyō (730), Lord Ōtomo Tabito,
> Commander of the Dazaifu, was suddenly
> stricken with a growth on his leg, and took to
> his bed and pillow in pain. He had an express
> messenger sent to the capital with a request to
> the Emperor that he be allowed to speak his
> last words to his half-brother Inakimi and his
> nephew Komaro. These two, Ōtomo Inakimi,
> Lieutenant in the Armory of the Right, and
> Ōtomo Komaro, Sub-Assistant in the Ministry
> of Ceremonies, were given fast steeds and
> ordered to hurry to Lord Ōtomo's side to
> attend his illness. Fortunately, however, after
> several weeks he recovered. Upon Lord
> Ōtomo's cure, Inakimi and Komaro left the
> Dazaifu and proceeded up to the capital. At
> this time Ōtomo Momoyo and Yamaguchi

Wakamaro, along with Lord Ōtomo's son
Yakamochi, sent express messengers to them.
When they all reached the horse station at
Hinamori, they held a banquet there with wine
and expressed their sorrows at parting with
these poems.

568-571

*Four poems by the Dazaifu officials as they banqueted
Lord Ōtomo Tabito, Commander of the Dazaifu, at the
horse station of Ashiki in the province of Chikuzen, as
he was on his way to the capital to assume the office of
Chancellor*

568

Lord who is in my thoughts
whether I sit or rise,
rise like the five hundred-fold waves
that break against the rocky shore
on the bends of the splendid cape.

> The above poem is by the Deputy
> Assistant Governor of Chikuzen,
> Kadobe Isotari.

569

Thoughts of you
are dyed into my heart,
like the purple that, they say,
the Chinese dye their robes with.

570

As the day approaches
when you, my Lord, set out
            for Yamato,
even the deer standing in the fields
give a cry that echoes mournfully.

> The above two poems are by the
> Scribe Asada Yasu.

571

Splendid is the moon,
and crystalline sounds the river's purl.
Come, let us all revel,
we who go to the capital
and we who stay behind.

> The above poem is by Ōtomo
> Yotsuna, Lieutenant of the frontier
> guardsmen.

572 and 573

*Two poems sent by the Priest Mansei to Lord Ōtomo
Tabito, Commander of the Dazaifu, after he had gone
up to the capital*

Left behind by my Lord,
whom I never tired to gaze upon,
as upon a true clear mirror,
now the mornings and the evenings
            find me desolate.

Though my pitch-black hair
            has turned white,

there still are times
when I fall into painful longing.

574 and 575

*Two poems by Lord Ōtomo Tabito, the Chancellor, in
response*

Where is Tsukushi now?
Over there, it seems,
    by the mountains
where the white clouds trail.

Like the cranes that search for food
among the reeds
    in the inlets of Kusaka Cove,
I stumble and falter,
now, without companion.

576

*Poem composed by Fujii Ōnari, Governor of Chikugo,
after Lord Ōtomo Tabito, Commander of the Dazaifu,
had gone up to the capital*

Dismal from now on,
the road over Ki Mountain—[12]
and I had always wanted to take it!

---

[12] From the Governor's residence in Chikugo Province one reached the
Dazaifu by crossing Ki Mountain (城山).

577

*Poem by Lord Ōtomo Tabito, the Chancellor, when he
sent a new ceremonial cloak to Prince Takayasu,
Director of the Tsu Administration Board*

Do not let any other
     wear my clothes,
no matter how you treat them—
even should they touch the hands
of the men of Naniwa,
who haul in the nets.

578

Poem by Ōtomo Miyori, in his grief over a parting

Oh the garden of the house
where I thought I would live
as long as heaven and earth endure!

579 and 580

*Two poems presented by Yo Myōgun to Ōtomo
Yakamochi*

Though time has hardly passed
since I gazed on you, my Lord,
it feels like months and years.

My Lord, whom I desired
to gaze on and attend
as closely as the roots of sedge
that grow upon the foothill-
trailing mountain!

581-584

Four poems by the elder maiden of the Ōtomo Sakanoue house, sent to Ōtomo Yakamochi in response to poems of his

581

As long as we are alive,
there is always a chance
          that we will meet.
Why, then did you appear in my dreams
to tell me, "Woman, let us die"?

582

Brave man, I realize
you have yearned for me,
but could your longing compare
to that in the heart
of a frail-limbed woman?

583

Is it because his feelings fade
as easily as the colors
dyed from dayflowers
that the man I long for
does not even send me word?

584

You, my Lord,
whom I long to see always:
the way no day passes
when the clouds that rise in the morning
over Kasuga Mountain
do not rest in the sky.

585

Poem by Lady Ōtomo Sakanoue

You can leave my house
        anytime you want,
but is it right for you to go
just when you are full of longing
                for your wife?

586

*Poem sent to the elder daughter of the Tamura house by
Ōtomo Inakimi*

> She was the daughter of Lord Ōtomo
> Sukunamaro.

If we had not met,
I never would have yearned for you.
But now that having seen you
fills me with such longing—
Oh what shall I do?

> The above poem was composed by
> her elder sister, Lady Sakanoue.

587-610

Twenty-four poems sent to Ōtomo Yakamochi by Lady Kasa

587

Look on my tokens,
  and remember me.
I too shall think of you
as the years trail long away
  like a strand of rough gems.

588

Pining in my wait for you,
  like the pines on Toba Mountain
  where the white bird flies,[13]
I have gone on longing
  through these months.

589

Not knowing
I am in Uchimi Village,
  where they pound their sleeves
  on the fulling block,
he does not come to see me,
though I wait for him.

---

[13] *Matsu* in the original is both "pine tree" and "to wait" (especially with longing or pining). This is a rare example of a Japanese pun "translatable" into English, which conveys (perhaps all too well) a sense of the artificial effect of a purely formal, i.e., homophonic link between two words in the *tanka*. This particular device, with no associative resonance other than the purely aural, seems to anticipate the extremely conscious word-play in poetry of the Heian Period.

590

You think it is all right
now that the years have trailed away
    like a strand of rough gems.
But no, my man, don't do it!
Never reveal my name!

591

Are my thoughts
    revealed to others?
I dreamed my jewelled comb box
was opened to the light.

592

Will I go on
merely hearing of you from afar—
        like the cranes that seem
            to cry in the dark night—
never meeting you?

593

Longing for you
leaves me helpless with despair;
I lean against a little pine
on Nara Mountain,
                        grieving.

594

Like the white dew fading
from the grass where sunset shimmers
          before my house,
my heart seems to dissolve
          in thoughts of you.

595

Could I ever forget you,
as long as my life be safe?
No, not even if my longing
     increases day by day.

596

Greater than the sands
on a beach it takes eight hundred
          days to cross
is my longing for you,
O guardian of the offshore island.

597

This world is thick with men's eyes,
and so I must go on longing for you,
          my Lord,
though you are as near to me
as the spaces in a bridge of stepping stones.

598

One may die from longing, too.
Like the hidden current
    in the Minase River,
unperceived, I grow thinner
        with each month,
        with each day.

599

Though we only saw each other
dimly through the morning mist,
I go on longing for you,
so much that I shall die.

600

I go on longing
for one as fearsome
as the waves on the Ise Sea
that break
and set the rocks to roaring.

601

Never, even in my heart,
        did I imagine it:
that I would long for you like this,
although no mountains,
        no rivers separate us.

602

When evening falls
my longing over things increases,
as an apparition of the one I met
comes speaking to me.

603

If longing were a thing
one could die from,
death would have come to me
          and come again
a thousand times!

604

I saw you in a dream,
girding your body
with your great sword.
What does this foretell?
Perhaps that I shall meet you.

605

Only if the gods
      of heaven and earth
            were without reason
would I die without meeting you,
Lord whom I long for.

606

I too shall think of him;
let him not forget.
Let there never be a time
when the winds cease to blow
          upon Tananowa Cove.[14]

607

I hear the tolling of the bell,
commanding everyone to sleep.
But I long for you, my Lord,
and cannot fall asleep.

608

To long for one
who does not long for you
is like kowtowing to hungry demons
          in the great temple
                    from behind.

609

Not even in my heart
did I imagine it:
that I would be returning
          once again
to my native village.

---

[14] This translation is based on Omodaka Hisataka's reconstruction of the traditionally unreadable third line, 多奈和丹 "*tanawani*," as 多奈乃和乃, "*tananowano*," the name of a place (presently Tannowa) on a cape south of Ōsaka facing Awaji Island. Other possible interpretations of 多奈和丹 include an adverb, now lost, dealing with the weather.

610

As long as you were near
I could live without seeing you,
but now that you
are farther and farther away,
I fear I cannot bear it.

> The last two poems above were sent
> to him after they had parted.

611 and 612

Two poems in response by Ōtomo Yakamochi

Is it because I fear
I cannot meet my woman again
that my breast is choked
with a dreadful sorrow?

Rather should I
have kept my silence and repose.
For what did I begin to see her
when I cannot tell her of this love?

613-617

Five poems sent to Ōtomo Yakamochi by Princess Yamaguchi

613

Not wanting others to see
that I long over things,
I find each day troubled
with half-stirred desire.
I cannot go on like this.

614

I weep and cry in vain
for one who does not love me,
until the tears
drench my white-cloth sleeves.

615

Even if, my man,
you do not think of me,
at least let me take your arms
    for my well-woven pillow
        in my dreams.

616

I do not sorrow that my name,
    like a great sword,
    be tarnished,
for the years have passed
without my meeting you.

617

Is it for the rising of desire—
    like the tide come spilling
    up from the reedy shore—
that I cannot forget you?

618

Poem sent by Lady Ōmiwa to Ōtomo Yakamochi

Plover calling your companion
in the depths of night,
crying in vain for me
at the hour I am fallen,
desolate, into longing.

619

A poem of reproach by Lady Ōtomo Sakanoue

    with tanka

You spoke to me
with feelings fine as the sedge
      at Naniwa,
where sunlight sweeps
      across the bay,
and told me we would be together
"deep and long, through the years,"
and so I yielded you my heart
    that I had burnished
    slick as a true, clear mirror.
Since that day
my mind has known no pitch and roll,
no seaweed's swaying with the waves.
And now that I trust in you,
as I would in a great ship—
    Oh is it the raging gods
    that rend us apart
    or is it the men of this world
    who obstruct you?—
my Lord, who came back and forth to me,

you cease to come.
And lately I do not even see
   your messenger,
    with his jewelled catalpa staff,
and I am helpless in my terrible despair.
All through the pitch-black nights
and through the days
till the red-trailing sun yields to dusk
I grieve,
    but there is no use,
I long,
    but there is nothing I can do.
Just as they say—
    "a frail-limbed woman"—
I wander about,
weeping and crying aloud like a child.
How long, I wonder, can I wait
      for your messenger?

620

Envoy

If you had not made me
place my trust in you,
promising me "forever,"
would I have fallen
into such longing?

621

Poem sent to Saeki Azumabito, Vice-Commander of the Military Supervisors of the Western Sea Route, by his wife

Is it because
my longing knows no pause
that I saw you in my dreams,
    my Lord who journeys
    with grass for pillow?

622

Poem by Saeki Azumabito in response

Because my journey,
  with grass for pillow,
    has turned long,
it is you I think of.
My woman, do not worry yourself
        with yearning.

623

Poem recited by Prince Ikebe at a banquet

Moonlight has shifted through the leaves
        of the pine in the garden.
Are you gone from me, O Lord,
like the yellow leaves of autumn?
So many are the nights we do not meet.

624

Poem by the Emperor, thinking of Princess Sakahito

> The Princess was the granddaughter
> of Prince Hozumi.

My woman who tells me
that just because we met on the road
and I gave her a smile,
now her longing will surely melt her away
       like the fallen snow!

625

Poem by Prince Takayasu when he sent a maiden a gift of wrapped silver carp

> Prince Takayasu later was bestowed
> the surname Ōhara no Mahito.

I have rowed out to the offing
and walked along the shore,
to catch for my woman
the little silver carp
that hide among the seaweed.

626

Poem presented to the Emperor by Princess Yashiro

Because of you, my Lord,
the talk flies thick about me.
I am going to the Asuka River,
       in my native village,
there to wash away the stains.

627

*Poem sent by a maiden in response to one by Saeki
Akamaro*

Brave man who wants to make
    a pillow of my sleeves,
first find yourself the waters of youth,
for white hairs have sprouted on your head.

628

Poem by Saeki Akamaro in response

I do not concern myself
with the white hairs sprouted on my head.
But somehow I shall find
the waters of youth,
        then go to you.

629

A banquet poem by Ōtomo Yotsuna

Why has your messenger come
when it is you yourself, my Lord—
    whatever your intention—
whom I can hardly wait to see?

630

Poem by Saeki Akamaro

The first blossom
is surely meant to fall.
But men's talk gathers
thick around her,
and she tends to hesitate.

631 and 632

Two poems sent by Prince Yuhara to a maiden

He was the son of Prince Shiki.

It seems she lacks
even outward courtesy,
as I think how she sent me back
on the long road home.

What shall I do with this woman
like the *katsura* tree in the moon[15]
that my eyes can see
but my hands cannot touch?

633 and 634

Two poems by the maiden in response

Was it because I longed for you
so intensely
that I saw you in my dreams
as I slept on my well-woven pillow
pushed to one side of the bed?

I envy your wife,
who is beside you as you journey,
with grass for pillow,
though you do not tire
to look on her at home.

---

[15] The *katsura* is the "Judas tree." The belief in its presence in the moon comes from Chinese legend.

635 and 636

Two more poems sent to her by Prince Yuhara

Yes, I have brought my wife
    on this journey,
        with grass for pillow,
but my thoughts are with the jewel
hidden in the box of combs.

I send you clothes
as a token of myself.
Keep them by your well-woven pillow
and wrap yourself in them
               when you sleep.

637

Another poem sent by the maiden in response

I will keep these clothes,
    a token of my man,
always beside me.
They will be our conjugal words,
though they cannot speak.

638

Another poem sent to her by Prince Yuhara

Only a night have we been apart,
and already my heart is torn
as if the days have threaded,
   like a strand of rough gems,
        into a month.

639

Another poem sent by the maiden in response

Is it because
he longs for me like this
that I see him in my dreams
through the pitch-black night
        and cannot sleep?

640

Another poem by Prince Yuhara

Alas! Though her village lies nearby,
must I go on longing for her
as if she dwelt among the clouds—
though a month has yet to pass?

641

Another poem by the maiden in response

Fearing that to tell me we are through
        would cause me misery,
you keep me tassled to your side,
like your swords with burnished blades.
But O my Lord, is this a happy thing?

642

Poem by Prince Yuhara

When I first loved you I determined
that if the longing twisted me in disarray
I would string my heart upon a loom
        to be unravelled.

643-645

Three poems of reproach by Lady Ki

> She was the daughter of Lord Kahito,
> and her personal name was Woshika.
> She married Prince Aki.

643

If I were a woman
who kept the order of this world,
I would not be crossing the Anase River,
        "the river to my man,"
that I cross now.

644

Misery takes me now
as I think of how I let you go,
you who were my very thread
        of vital breath.

645

The day approaches
when our white-cloth sleeves
        must pull apart;
my heart is choked with sorrow,
I weep and cry aloud.

646

Poem by Ōtomo Surugamaro

A brave man
but, desolate with longing,
he grieves time and time again.
And you refuse to bear
the burden of his grief.

647

Poem by Lady Ōtomo Sakanoue

Not a single day
do I forget you in my heart.
But you, my Lord, are one
who gathers gossip thick about you.

648

Poem by Ōtomo Surugamaro

The days have turned long
since we stopped meeting.
And I worry, O my woman,
if these days
find you well and happy.

649

Poem by Lady Ōtomo Sakanoue

They never ceased,
your messenger's arrivals
and the summer vines.
But now he no longer comes,

and I have wondered
if something has occurred.

> Lady Ōtomo Sakanoue was the
> daughter of Lord Ōtomo Yasumaro,
> the Saho Chancellor. Surugamaro
> was the grandson of Lord Ōtomo
> Miyuki, the Great Lord of Takechi.
> Since the two lords were brothers, the
> daughter of one and the grandson of
> the other were aunt and nephew.
> Therefore they composed poems and
> sent them to each other, inquiring of
> one another's welfare.

650

*Poem by Ōtomo Miyori in his delight at meeting a
woman again after having parted from her*

It seems my girl
has been dwelling
in the land of immortals,
for she is younger now
than when I saw her last.

651 and 652

Two poems by Lady Ōtomo Sakanoue

Dew and frost from the distant heavens
remain now to cover the earth;
and the ones you left at home,
they too must long for you as they wait.

My precious jewel has been received
      into its owner's hands
and I must endure it.
Now let me sleep
      with my pillow for companion.

653-655

Three poems by Ōtomo Surugamaro

653

Though in my heart
I have not forgotten you,
so many days have slipped away
without my seeing you, and now
a month has passed.

654

If I tell you I long for you
though a month has yet to pass
        since we saw each other,
will you think me rash?

655

If I told you I love you
when I do not love you,
the gods of heaven and earth
would find me out.[16]

---

[16] This is followed by an undecipherable fifth phrase, 邑礼左変.

656-661

Six poems by Lady Ōtomo Sakanoue

656

I am the one who feels it,
this longing for you, my man.
For you to say you long for me
is merely a solace of words.

657

I vowed not to think of you
but oh my heart, so changeable
like the colors
        of the flowering almond!

658

Though I know there is no use
                thinking of you,
why do I go on so intensely
                yearning for you?

659

Already the gossip
is thick about us;
if we go on like this—
        O my man!—
what awaits us at the end?

660

Others are trying
to rend me from you.
My Lord, do not listen
to their slander!

661

I have longed and longed for you,
and now that we have met, if only now,
expend on me your tender words,
if you think our love will last.

662

Poem by Prince Ichihara

In my dreams I saw the child
tossing her little fishing net
on the waters of Cape Sade,
hidden in the shadows
of Ago's five-hundred-folded mountains.

663

Poem by Ato Toshitari

O my beloved little wife
    so dear to me
like the voices of the birds
    crying by my house
as they fly across the Saho River ford.

664

Poem by Ōtomo Katami

Even if the rains fell
  at Furu, by Isonokami,[17]
how could they keep me inside
when I have vowed to my woman
  that we shall meet?

665

Poem by Abe Mushimaro

I never tired to gaze upon her
when we sat and faced each other;
now my girl is rising,
intent on leaving me,
and I do not know what to do.

666 and 667

Two poems by Lady Ōtomo Sakanoue

It has not been so long
since we saw each other,
yet how intensely do I
go on yearning for you!

I longed and yearned,
and finally I have met you.
Now the moon is there above us,

---

[17] *Furu* is both a place name and the verb "to fall" (of rain, snow, etc.).

the night still wraps us deep.
Wait with me a while before you go.

> The mother of Lady Ōtomo
> Sakanoue, Inner Mistress Ishikawa,
> and the mother of Abe Mushimaro,
> Outer Mistress Azumi,[18] were sisters
> living in the same household, sharing
> the intimacy of close blood-relations.
> Because of this, Lady Sakanoue and
> Mushimaro were not kept from
> seeing each other, and from the time
> of their youth had already spoken
> with each other on personal terms.
> Here they carry out a playful dialog
> composing poems and sending them
> to each other.

668

Poem by Prince Atsumi

My thoughts of you
do not easily pass, my Lord,
like white clouds
over mountains bright with color
in the morning and throughout the day.

669

Poem by Prince Kasuga

> He was the son of Prince Shiki; his
> mother was called Princess Taki.

Show your feelings clearly,
like the color of the oranges that grow

---

[18] "Inner Mistress" is *Uchi no Myōbu*, the title given a woman herself holding the fifth court rank or above. "Outer Mistress" is *Ge no Myōbu*, the title given a woman whose husband holds the fifth court rank or above.

upon the foothill-trailing mountains,
so that we may go on with our exchanges
and perhaps even meet.

670

Poem by Prince Yuhara

Come to me by moonlight.
There is no foothill-trailing
mountains' distance between us.

671

Poem in response

> The name of the author is yet
> unclear.

The moon's crystal gleam
     illuminates the way,
but my heart is confused
     and my desire knows no resolve.

672

Poem by Abe Mushimaro

Why do I go on longing for you,
go on with this insignificant life
like a wristband woven
in simple Yamato patterns?

673 and 674

Two poems by Lady Ōtomo Sakanoue

If I yielded you my heart
    that I have burnished
    slick as a true clear mirror,
it will be no use
if later I should speak regrets.

Your words say you will love me
now and in the time to come,
like a strand of true jewels.
But regrets will be of no use
after I have met you.

675-679

*Five poems sent by Lady Nakatomi to Ōtomo
Yakamochi*

675

Like the iris
    growing in the marsh of Saki,
where the maiden flowers bloom,
I find myself longing
in a way I have never known.[19]

---

[19] The "maidenflowers" are *ominaeshi* (娘子部四), "*patrinia scabiosaefolia.*"
It is their "bloom" (*saki*) which homophonically introduces the place name
Saki.

676

I shall meet you, my Lord,
whom I love as deeply
as the bottommost depths of the ocean—
even if it takes years.

677

It seems I long for one
I do not know at all,
my heart dimmed with sorrow
like the clouds
that cling through the morning
to Kasuga Mountain.

678

Only if I could meet you
            in the flesh
and see you, only then
would longing cease its hold
on my soul-swollen life.

679

If you refuse I shall not force you
but shall go on longing, my man,
with thoughts torn in thin little strands
            like the roots of sedge.

680-682

Three poems by Ōtomo Yakamochi, upon parting from a friend

680

It must be because
you listen to others' slander
that, though I wait for you, my Lord,
                    intensely,
you do not come.

681

If rather our friendship ended,
would I now be yearning like this,
making you the thread
              of my vital breath?

682

I who long for him
though he does not think of me:
with all my heart consumed,
with each tiny fiber exhausted.

683-689

Seven poems by Lady Ōtomo Sakanoue

683

This is a land of fearful gossip!
Do not show your emotion,
do not be revealed in scarlet hues,
even if the longing kills you.

684

O my man, let me die now!
For even while I live
no one tells me
you wish to draw your heart to me.

685

Is it for the thickness of men's gossip
that you stay there, longing for me,
our houses separate
like swords in a twin sheath?[20]

686

Do I really think a thousand years
have come and gone in these few days,
or is it merely my desire to see you?

[20] The Shōsōin Collection includes "swords in a triple sheath" and "swords in a ten-fold sheath," and the "twin sheath" is thought to be a similar object. The swords are bundled together but each is in its own separate sheath, thus a metaphorical vehicle for the two houses close to each other yet separated by the sheath of gossip.

687

This cherishing heart
is a quick river
that, stopped
      and stopped again,
yet shall burst its dams.

688

Don't let the smiles we exchange
be revealed to the eyes of men
clearly as the clouds
which course across blue mountains.

689

No seas or mountains
     lie between us,
yet why are our meetings
such a meager few,
     and only for a glance,
     for a word?

690

Poem by Ōtomo Miyori, in his sorrow over a parting

The gleaming sun
is darkness in my eyes;
the tears drench my clothes,
there is no one here to dry them.

691 and 692

Two poems sent to a maiden by Ōtomo Yakamochi

Though many are the courtiers
    of the great palace—
      its ramparts thick with stone—
she is the one
    who has seized my heart.

The way my woman lacks in courtesy!
As I think how she exhausts
      so many hearts of men.

693

Poem by Ōtomo Chimuro

    The facts about him are yet unclear.

Thus have I gone on longing,
my thoughts of you never passing:
    like the clouds that trail
    over the fields of Akitsu.

694 and 695

Two poems by Princess Hirokawa

    She was the granddaughter of Prince
    Hozumi, and the daughter of Prince
    Kamitsumichi

This longing comes
from my very heart,
the grass of longing
pitched high in seven carts,
in seven mighty carts.

Never again
would longing befall me,
             I thought;
but where does this longing come from
that has me in its clutches now?

696

Poem by Ishikawa Hironari

>   He later was bestowed the surname
>   Takamado no Ason

Could this longing
for the ones at home
             ever cease,
now that the years are passing
       here in the village of Izumi,
       where the frogs sing?

697-699

Three poems by Ōtomo Katami

697

Do not speak of him
             that I may hear;
it is my Lord's true presence
that tears my heart with desire,
like rushes scythed from roots.

698

Thicker and thicker
like morning clouds that linger
    over the fields of Kasuga,
so my longing grows
      with each new month,
      with each new day.

699

Like the waters diverted
a thousand times in a single rapid
only to stream together later,
so we too shall meet,
even if not right away.

700

*Poem composed by Ōtomo Yakamochi upon arriving at
a maiden's gate*

So it is true
that I must withdraw like this,
back down the road
    which was not so short
up which I struggled to your house?

701 and 702

Two poems sent to Ōtomo Yakamochi by the maiden Momoe of Kawachi

I met him
but a slight moment.
On what day,
   on what kind of day
will I see him again,
   if only from afar?

To this day I have not forgotten
the moon on that pitch-black night,
for my thoughts of you
               have known no lull.

703 and 704

Two poems by the maiden Kamunagibe Maso

Since that day
   when I met my man
      until this day
not for a moment
   have the tears
      dried from my sleeves.

I have desired
   life to be as long
      as a rope of mulberry
because I want to look upon you,
      never ceasing.

705

Poem sent to a young girl by Ōtomo Yakamochi

I see the girl in my dreams,
wearing now the wreath of feathers;
have I been longing for her
           deep within my heart?[21]

706

Poem sent by the young girl in response

There is no girl here
who wears now the wreath of feathers;
which girl can it be
you long for so intensely?

707 and 708

*Two poems sent to Ōtomo Yakamochi by the maiden
Awatame*

No way to dispel this grief,
I have fallen
        into unrequited longing:
the bottom of a lidless pot.

Is there no way
for us to meet again?
Next time I shall hold you
        with sorcery
to my white-cloth sleeves.

---

[21] The "wreath of feathers" is thought to have been a ceremonial deco-
ration by which a girl was festooned upon reaching adulthood.

709

Poem by the maiden Ōyakeme of the land of Buzen

Dim lies the road
    in the evening darkness.
Wait for the moon, my man,
      before you go,
that I may look upon you until then.

710

Poem by the maiden Ato Tobira

He has appeared in my dreams,
the one with whom
    I stole a second's glance
by the light of the moon
as it coursed the splendid sky.

711-713

Three poems by the maiden Ōme of Taniwa

711

I do not love you
with a capricious heart,
not like the fallen leaves
floating on this pond
    where the ducks play.

712

Is it a sin?
Have I touched the cedar
hallowed by the priests of Miwa,
             Miwa of sweet wine,
that meeting you should be so hard?

713

Oh these days
when my man hears rumors—
rumors rising like a lofty fence—
and his heart falters,
and I cannot meet him!

714-720

Seven poems sent to a maiden by Ōtomo Yakamochi

714

I have gone on longing for you
                    in my heart,
but there is no way to meet you
and I can only sigh from afar.

715

When can I make my way to you,
urging my horse
     across the crystal shallows
             of the Saho ford,
                   where the plover cries?

BY ISHIKAWA TADAYUKI

Nara: the Saho River

When can I make my way to you,
urging my horse
    across the crystal shallows
        of the Saho ford,
            where the plover cries?

    Ōtomo Yakamochi (one of "Seven poems sent to a
    maiden," IV.715)

716

Might it possibly
  have appeared to you
      in your dreams,
my heart that longs for you
unmindful of day and night?

717

Such misery
that I should love unrequited
one without the least regard for me!

718

Astonished,
I see my woman smiling
      in my dream,
and feel the fire
burning on inside my heart.

719

Am I, who thought
I was a brave man,
to fall like this,
gaunt and haggard,
into unrequited longing?

720

Can she not know
that I long for her like this,
rending my heart,
tearing these twines of inner flesh?

721

Poem presented to the Emperor Shōmu

> Composed by Lady Ōtomo
> Sakanoue, at her mansion in the Saho
> Hills

Here I am among the foothill-
                    trailing mountains,
where there are no courtly graces,
so I pray you do not rebuke me
                    for my ways.

722

Poem by Ōtomo Yakamochi

Instead of yearning for you
                    like this,
I wish I could have been
                    a rock or tree,
never cursed with longing.

723

*Poem sent by Lady Ōtomo Sakanoue from the rice fields
of Tomi to her daughter, the elder maiden of the
Sakanoue house, who had stayed at home*

    with tanka

Though I did not venture
    to some far eternal land,
you stood by the gate,
        my daughter,
with such sorrow on your face
that thinking of you,
unmindful of day
    and pitch-black night,
has turned my body gaunt.
When I sigh for you
my very sleeves are wet with tears.
When I long for you
    in vain like this,
I feel I cannot bear to stay
    here in my native village
    even this single month.

724

Envoy

Is it because, my little girl,
    you long for me,
with your thoughts dissheveled
    like your morning hair,
that I saw you in my dreams?

725 and 726

Two poems presented to the Emperor Shōmu

> Composed by Lady Ōtomo Sakanoue
> in the village of Kasuga

O waters in the pond
where the grebes dive,
if you have sympathy
reveal to my Lord
  this heart of mine
  that longs for him.

Instead of longing for you
     from afar,
would that I were the duck
they tell me lives in the pond
    by your house, my Lord.

727 and 728

*Two poems sent to the elder daughter of the Sakanoue
house by Ōtomo Yakamochi*

> After having separated for several
> years, the two of them met again and
> exchanged poems.

I fastened day lilies,
"grasses of forgetfulness,"
to the belt of my trousers,
but the worthless weeds
brought oblivion only in name.[22]

---

[22] Day lilies are *wasuregusa* ("grasses of forgetfulness").

Is there, I wonder,
a land where no one lives?
I would take my woman by the hand
and dwell there beside her.

729-731

*Three poems sent to Ōtomo Yakamochi by the elder
daughter of the Ōtomo Sakanoue house*

729

If you were a jewel
I would wrap you round my wrist,
but you are a man, you belong
to this world of the living,
and it is hard
        to wrap you round my wrist.

730

Any night we could have met,
then why did we meet
on that particular evening,
giving rise to gossip so thick!

731

Let my name be stained
    five hundred times,
    a thousand times.
But if your name, my Lord,
be bandied in their gossip,
I would weep with regret!

732-734

Three more poems by Ōtomo Yakamochi in response

732

Now I no longer
have regrets about my name,
be it gossiped of
          a thousand times—
if the gossip is
because of you, my woman.

733

Can the realm of life
come to us twice?
Then why must I sleep alone,
unable to meet my woman?

734

Instead of these yearnings,
Oh that I could be a jewel
and truly wrapped
around my woman's wrist!

735

*A poem sent to Ōtomo Yakamochi by this same elder
daughter of the Sakanoue house*

On the night
when the mists trail
over Kasuga Mountain

and the moon glimmers dimly,
my heart clouded over,
will I be sleeping alone?

736

*Another poem by Ōtomo Yakamochi in response to the
elder daughter of the Sakanoue house*

On the moonlit night
I came out and stood by my gate,
and performed evening sorcery
and performed sorcery of feet—[23]
desiring to go to you.

737 and 738

*Two poems sent to Ōtomo Yakamochi by this same
elder daughter of the Sakanoue house*

People may say this and that,
but let us meet again, my Lord,
       despite them,
meet later, like Nochise Mountain
       on the road to Wakasa.[24]

This world seems a thing of pain
as I realize I love you so much
that I cannot bear the longing,
       that it will kill me.

---

[23] "Evening sorcery"—see Book Three, note 12. "Sorcery of feet" is unclear. Nakanishi Susumu suggests a method of fortune-telling by which one walked a certain set distance and made a judgment according to whether it was reached on the left or right foot.
[24] The "*nochi*" in "*Nochise*" means "later."

739 and 740

Two more poems by Yakamochi in response to the elder daughter of the Sakanoue house

Only the hope
that later we shall meet again
      like Nochise Mountain
has kept me alive until today,
though the longing should have killed me.

How she makes me
      trust her completely
      with her mere words
promising to meet me later,
but I suspect
      she will not meet me.

741-755

Fifteen more poems sent to the elder daughter of the Sakanoue house by Ōtomo Yakamochi

741

Painful was the rendezvous
we had in my dream;
awakening, I reached for you
but my hands could not touch you.

742

The belt that you, my woman,
wrapped once around my waist
I must wrap three times now,
so gaunt has yearning made me.

743

Let my longing be as great
as seven boulders
each a thousand men must haul
all hung upon my neck—
I leave it to the gods.

744

When evening comes
I shall open the door to my house
                              and wait,
in preparation for the one
who told me in my dreams
that she would come to see me.

745

Though I should always see you,
    even should I see you
    in the morning and the evening too,
will I still long for you
as if I never see you?

746

Never in my life
have I seen such a marvellous thing,
this bag you wove for me
with such pleasure
that it leaves me speechless.

747

I shall wear your robe,
          this token of you,
beneath my clothes.
How could I ever take it off
until we meet face to face again?

748

Let me die of longing—
it would be all the same.
For what have I been pained
by the eyes of men,
the words of others?

749

Even if I only see her
          in my dreams
I could go on living;
does her total absence from my sight
mean I must die from longing?

750

My desire had died,
I passed the time in quiet loneliness.
But then what compelled me to begin again
these half-hearted rendezvous
          that bring such pain?

751

Though several days
have yet to pass
since we saw each other,
how intensely I long for her,
driving madness upon madness!

752

What can I do
when she bears on my mind like this,
mere visions of her obsessing me?
What can I do
inside the thicket of men's eyes?

753

I thought that, after we had met,
my desire would be assuaged a while,
but now my longing rages all the more.

754

A vision of my woman
appears before me:
sunken into longing
when I came out from her house
as night yielded to wisps of dawn.

755

As the times grow many
when I must come out from her house
as night yields to wisps of dawn,
it makes my breast
          feel gashed and set afire.

756-759

*Four poems sent to the elder daughter of the Sakanoue
house by the elder daughter of the Ōtomo Tamura house*

756

It is painful
to long for you from afar.
Plan it, my girl,
so that we may continue
          to see each other.

757

If you were far away
I could bear this misery,
yet being unable to see you
leaves me helpless in despair.

758

Oh for a way to see the woman
to whom my anticipation soars
like lofty mountains
where the white clouds trail!

759

What kind of day will it be
when I may escort you, woman,
into my shabby hut
overgrown with goose grass?

> The elder daughter of the Tamura
> house and the elder daughter of the
> Sakanoue house were both daughters
> of Lord Ōtomo Sukunamaro, the
> Councillor of the Right. The lord's
> residence was in the village of
> Tamura, and thus his daughter was
> called the elder daughter of the
> Tamura house. Her sister's mother,
> however, had her residence in the
> village of Sakanoue, and thus her
> sister was called the elder daughter of
> the Sakanoue house. The sisters had
> occasion to inquire of each other's
> welfare, and thus exchanged these
> poems.

760 and 761

*Two poems sent by Lady Ōtomo Sakanoue from the rice
fields of Takeda to her daughter*

I gaze out
over the fields of Takeda
and see the cranes that cry there
           without interval,
           without pause:
such is my longing for you.

Oh my child
who loved me helplessly
like a hovering bird
over quick river shallows!

762 and 763

Two poems sent to Ōtomo Yakamochi by Lady Ki

> The Lady's personal name was
> Woshika.

I do not tell you, "No,
I am too old and wizened,"
but only fear that later
it will bring me lonely sorrow.

If we keep it loosely tied,
our bond,
        this strand of jewels,
how could we fail to meet later?

764

Poem by Ōtomo Yakamochi in response

Even if you turn a hundred,
with your old tongue
                drooping out
and your back stooped,
I shall not despise you,
though the longing may grow.

765

*Poem composed by Ōtomo Yakamochi while in the
capital at Kuni, thinking of the elder daughter of the
Sakanoue house who had remained at her home in Nara*

Though but a single fold
of mountains separates us,
does the splendor of the moon
call my woman out to her gate,
where she stands waiting for me?

766

Poem by Lady Fujiwara in immediate response upon
hearing this

The road is distant,
and I realize you will not come,
yet I shall go on waiting
                    as you say,
desiring your eyes upon me.

767 and 768

Two more poems sent by Ōtomo Yakamochi to the elder
daughter of the Sakanoue house

Is it because
the road to the capital is distant
that, though you go to sleep these nights
                    with pledges to me,
you do not appear in my dreams?

Here in the capital at Kuni,
where our Lord rules anew,
long the time has passed
since I have met my woman.
Quickly I would go to see her.

769

Poem sent by Ōtomo Yakamochi in response to Lady Ki

Alone on the mountainside
on a day when the rains
fall from the distant heavens,
I am overcome with gloom.

770-774

*Five poems sent by Ōtomo Yakamochi from the capital
at Kuni to the elder daughter of the Sakanoue house*

770

It is only because
the eyes of men are many
that I have not met you,
not that I have forgotten you
even within my heart.

771

Even the lies you tell
   sound believeable;
do you truly long for me
        in reality?

772

Though I undo my sash,
hoping, at least, to see you
        in my dreams,

yet I go on longing,
   unable to meet you.
You are truly invisible!

773

Even among dumb trees
are born capricious flowers
    like the hydrangea;
I have been deceived
by the slick words of Moroto.

774

Though she tells me
  a million times
    that she loves me,
I shall not put faith
in the slick words of Moroto.

775

Poem sent by Ōtomo Yakamochi to Lady Ki

Though I have thought of her
since my years in Nara—
  that ancient ruined town
  where the quail cry—
why is there no way
for me to meet my woman?

776

Poem sent by Lady Ki to Ōtomo Yakamochi in response to his

Who was it spoke the first word?
But now your passion trickles to a halt
like water that stagnates in the ricebeds
        halfway down the hillside.

777-781

Five more poems sent by Ōtomo Yakamochi to Lady Ki

777

If I went to see the hedge
in front of my girl's house,
I wonder if I might not
be turned back at the gate?

778

Can it be simply the desire
to examine the hedge
that makes me want to go?
No, my Lord, it is to see you.[25]

779

Leave them to me,
the black logs you need

---

[25] It is not unusual to find personal exchange poems addressed to both the same and the opposite sex within a single set. Here, in a set specifically addressed to Lady Ki, Yakamochi's addressing her as a man seems to be a playful joke.

to plank your roof.
I am near the mountains,
I will gather
and bring them tomorrow.

780

Though I serve you,
    gathering black logs
        and cutting grass,
I expect no praise from you,
not even to be called
        your diligent slave.

781

Last night,
that pitch-black night,
you sent me back.
Do not send me back
this evening too,
back on the distant road.

782

Poem sent to a friend, along with a present, by Lady Ki

    The Lady's personal name was
    Woshika.

Winds roared through the lofty sky
and churned across the beach,
but oh the sleek seaweed
I cut for you, my woman,
drenched to my very sleeves!

783-785

Three poems sent by Ōtomo Yakamochi to a maiden

783

Though I have longed for you
from the year before last
        until this year,
why is it so hard
        to meet you, woman?

784

There is nothing more
I can say in reality;
if I could only dream
that I sleep pillowed in her arms!

785

I no more begrudge
the fading of my life
than that of the dew lying white
upon the grass by my house—
for I cannot meet my woman.

786-788

Three poems sent to Fujiwara Kusumaro by Ōtomo Yakamochi

786

The spring rains
 gather incessant force,
but your plum tree
 has yet to blossom—
because of its terrible youth?

787

I feel as if in a dream:
your messenger comes
so many times,
 O my beloved Lord!

788

I plant a plum tree,
the tips of whose branches
are so young and tender
that it cannot come to flower.
And men's words gather thick around it,
 troubling my heart.

789 and 790

*Two more poems sent by Yakamochi to Fujiwara
Kusumaro*

Somehow a murky haze
steals upon my heart,
as your messages come
at a time when spring mists trail.

I shall bide my time until—
    O herald gusts of spring!—
        you clearly speak;
if not now, my Lord,
        whenever you desire.

791 and 792

Two poems by Fujiwara Kusumaro in response

Do I not love her too
with feelings fine and intricate
as the roots of sedge
growing in the shade of crags
        among inland mountains?

It seems to be waiting
        for the spring rains;
the young plum tree by my house
        is still in bud.

BOOK FIVE

BY ISHIKAWA TADAYUKI

Nara: The Yakushiji pagoda, with the hills of Kasuga in the distance

POEMS ON VARIOUS THEMES

793

*Poem by Lord Ōtomo Tabito, Commander of the
Dazaifu, in response to the dreadful news that his wife
had died*[1]

Afflictions pile one upon another, and dreadful news
gathers in a heap. I am constantly filled with sadness
enough to rend the heart, and alone I weep gut-wrenching
tears. Only because of the great assistance the two of you
have given me have I somehow been able to keep my aged
body alive.

> My brush is unable to express all
> I wish to say—the grief of ancient
> and modern alike.

When I realize
this world is an empty thing,
then all the more I feel
a deeper and deeper sorrow.

> The sixth month, twenty-third day, of
> the fifth year of Jinki (728)

[1] The original merely has "dreadful news" (凶問). There is a question as to
whose death this refers to. Omodaka Hisataka sees a sequence of Tabito being
informed of the "dreadful news" of the death of Okura's wife, his responding
to it with poem no. 793, then poem no. 794 to be Okura's expression of his
own bereavement. Nakanishi Susumu, on the other hand, interprets the
"dreadful news" as that of the death of Tabito's own wife, with 793 as an
expression of Tabito's bereavement, followed by 794 as Okura's elegiac
offering of a poem of bereavement *for Tabito*. We are clearly in the realm of
biographical conjecture without biographical evidence. If one must make a
choice, it seems to me that the "dreadful news" indeed refers to the death of
Tabito's wife, if only because Tabito's Preface to 793 strikes me as an
expression of helplessness in the face of personal bereavement. This should be
regarded, however, as only a tentative choice.

794

Thus have I heard: that the birth and death of the four modes of life[2] are comparable to the emptiness of all dreams, that the course of life through the three realms[3] is like the endless spin of a cycle. Thus even the Elder Vimalakirti suffered the afflictions of pestilence in his priestly chamber, and even the great Sakyamuni could not stay the agonies of extinction as he sat in the sal forest. Thus we know that even the two greatest of saints were unable to deter Strongman Death from his visit. Who in the three thousand worlds[4] has ever been able to escape from the intent clutch of darkness?

Day and night scramble away like a pair of racing rats. Life is the zip of a bird across the eyes—it can fly away in a single morning. The elements devour each other like four wrestling snakes. Man's existence is no more than the flash of a white steed across the evening as glimpsed through a crevice in a wall. Oh how painful it is! The maiden's crimson face is gone forever with the woman's three duties to obey, and young white flesh is destroyed forever with the wife's four virtues.[5] Who ever expects the vows of husband and wife, that they shall be together until old age, to be betrayed, that one of them should be robbed of his mate halfway down the road of life, like a bird in solitary flight?

---

[2] In Buddhism, the modes of life: life born from the womb, life hatched from eggs, life born from moisture, life born by metamorphosis.

[3] In Buddhism, the modes of existence: the world of desire, the world of matter, the world of non-matter.

[4] In Buddhism, the immense breadth of the universe: One "world" is existence as it expands infinitely from the central point of Mount Sumera. Three thousand such "worlds."

[5] "The woman's three duties to obey": in Confucianism, the woman's duties to obey her father before marriage, her husband after marriage, and her son after her husband's death.

"The wife's four virtues": in Confucianism, for the wife to be chaste in her conduct, to be circumspect in her speech, to be graceful in her appearance, and to be skillful at handicrafts.

To no purpose were screens set up around the Orchid Chamber, our nuptial suite—the gut-wrenching sorrow grows ever more painful. In vain was the bright mirror hung above her pillow—tears gather in a falling stream, enough to dye bamboo. Once the gate to the Underworld is shut, there is no way for us to meet again. Oh how sad it is!

Waves on the river of love already collapsed,
and agony never to thicken again over the sea of pain;
I have always despised this tainted earth,
my constant wish to entrust my life to the Pure Land
                                        beyond.

A Japanese Lament

She came yearning after me,
   like a child in tears,
to the land of Tsukushi—
   Tsukushi
         of the white weaving—
to our Lord's distant Kyushu Court.
But before she could even
         catch her breath,
though months and years
         have yet to pass—
   so suddenly it shocks
            my very heart—
she has collapsed,
            swaying,
            on her death bed.
I do not know what to say,
            what to do.
I do not know how to ask
      the rocks and trees!

If she had been at home,
at least I would have
                    her mortal form.
How cruel that my revered wife—
        what could she
                    intend of me?—
should betray the emotions we felt
when we spoke to each other
        standing side by side
        like a pair of grebes,
and desert our home!

795-799

Envoys

795

What will it avail me
        to return home?
The marriage room
where our pillows lie together
will surely cause me desolation.

796

Helplessness of the heart:
how my woman—
        Oh my beloved!—
came yearning after me,
and only for this!

797

How I regret it!
If I had only known

it would come to this,
I would have shown her every corner
of this beautiful land.

798

The sandalwood blossoms
that my wife once gazed on
seem to fall and scatter,
while the tears I weep
        have yet to dry.

799

Mists rise and spread
over Ono Mountain;
mists rise and spread
in the wind of my sighs.

*The seventh month, twenty-first day, of the
    fifth year of Jingi
Presented by Yamanoue Okura, the Governor of
    Chikuzen*

800

Poem to set a confused heart straight

Preface

There is a certain type of man who knows he should
honor his father and mother, but forgets to discharge his
filial duties with devotion. He does not concern himself

with his wife and children, but treats them more lightly
than a pair of discarded shoes. He styles himself Professor
Disdain. Though his spirit may soar free among the blue
clouds, his body still remains among the dust of this world.
He shows no sign of being a sage who has undergone ascetic
discipline and mastered the Way. Perhaps he is one of the
tribe that wanders lost among the mountains and marshes.[6]
Thus, in order to show him the Three Bonds of Obligation[7]
and, further, to enlighten him as to the Five Teachings,[8] I
have sent him a poem, trying to set his confused heart
straight. My poem:

When you look
    at your father and mother,
        they are noble;
when you look
    at your wife and children,
          they are precious and lovely—
such is the natural way of the world.
Like birds in lime
we may struggle
but cannot escape it:
our own directions lie
beyond our knowing.
You who go off,
discarding your family
    as you would kick away

[6] Apparently there actually was a social problem of people abandoning the
homes and occupations they were officially registered under and wandering
"among the mountains and marshes." It was prevalent enough to have been
outlawed by an imperial decree in the fourth year of Keiun (707).

[7] In Confucianism, the bonds between lord and vassal, father and son, and
husband and wife.

[8] In Confucianism, the teachings for the father to be righteous, for the
mother to be compassionate, for the elder brother to be amicable, for the
younger brother to be obedient, and for the son to be filial. Both the Three
Bonds and the Five Teachings appear in the Preface to the Chinese poem
preceding poem no. 897.

a shoe with a hole in it,
are you a man
or are you born from rocks and trees?
Tell me your name!
Once you go to heaven,
you may do as you please;
here on earth, our Sovereign reigns.
Here beneath the gleaming sun and moon,
as far as the ends of the earth
where the clouds trail from the heavens,
as far as the far side of the valley
for the leaping toad,
he reigns.
And in this land,
   this splendid land,
can it be right
for you to do this and that,
   just as you please?

801

Envoy

It is a long road
   to distant heaven;
go home now, meekly,
and attend to your work.

802

Poem on thinking of his children

Preface

Sakyamuni expounds truthfully from his golden mouth,
"I love all things equally, the way I love my child Rāhula."
He also teaches us, "No love is greater than the love for

one's child." Even the greatest of saints cherishes his child. Who, then, among the living creatures of this world could fail to love his children?

When I eat a melon,
I think of my children.
When I eat chestnuts,
I long for them even more.
Where do they possibly come from?
Their mischief flickers
        before my eyes
and keeps me from my sleep.

803

Envoy

What do I need
        with silver,
        with gold and gems?
Could the most precious jewel
        be equal to my child?

804

Poem sorrowing on the impermanence of life in this world

Preface

Easy to gather and difficult to dispel are the eight great hardships.[9] Difficult to fully enjoy and easy to expend are the pleasures of life's century span. So the ancients lamented, and so today our grief finds the same cause. There-

---

[9] In Buddhism, birth, old age, sickness, death, separation, emotions of anger, the pain of non-attainment, and the pain of the five passions.

fore I have composed a poem, and with it hope to dispel
the sorrow of my black hair marked with white. My poem:

Our helplessness in this life
is like the streaming away
of the months and years.
Again and again
misfortune tracks us down
and assaults us with a hundred ills.
We cannot hold time
   in its blossoming:
          when young girls,
to be maidenly,
wrapped Chinese jewels
around their wrists
and, hand in hand
with companions of their age,
must once have played.
When has frost fallen
on hair as black
as the guts of river snails?
From where do wrinkles come
to crease those crimson faces?
We have let time go.
      Once strong young men,
to be manly,
girt their waists
with great swords
and, tossing saddles
with cloth embroidered
   in Yamato patterns
on their red-maned steeds,
mounted and rode for sport—
how could it last forever?
Few were the nights

I pushed apart the wooden doors
that young girls creak open and shut
and, groping to their side,
slept arm in jewelled arm,
arm in truly jewelled arm!
But now I walk
with a cane gripped in my hand
and propped against my waist.
Going this way,
    I am despised.
Going that way,
    I am hated.
Such, it seems,
is the fate of old men.
Though I regret the passing
of my life,
    that swelled with spirit,
there is nothing I can do.

805

Envoy

Like the unchanging cliffs,
I would remain just as I am.
But I am living in this world
and cannot hold time back.

*Poems 800-805 selected in Kamano County on the
twenty-first day of the seventh month, the fifth year of
Jinki (728). By Yamanoue Okura, the Governor of
Chikuzen.*

806 and 807

Two poems by Lord Ōtomo Tabito, Commander of the Dazaifu[10]

Humbly I received your letter, and knew with every word the noble purport of your message. Immediately I was struck with a longing so strong as to reach across the Milky Way, and my heart was racked with the pain of waiting, enough to make me embrace the bridge pillar.[11] I only hope that you encounter no hindrances in your comings and goings, and I await the time when a parting of the clouds may reveal to me your illustrious visage.

Would I could obtain
a dragon steed right now,
so I could fly
    to the capital at Nara,
    beautiful in blue earth.

There is no way for us
to meet in reality,
so come before my dreaming eyes
night after pitch-black night!

808 and 809

Two poems in response

I will find a dragon steed
for the one who wants to come
    to the capital at Nara,
    beautiful in blue earth.

[10] In the original, this ascription of authorship appears after the letter.

[11] An allusion to the Chinese legend in which a man by the name of Wei Sheng waited in vain for a woman beneath a bridge. Even when the water rose he refused to leave. Finally he drowned clinging to the bridge pillar.

Many the times
I cannot meet you face to face;
let us see each other
in our dreams at least,
each time we sleep
on our finely-woven pillows.

810 and 811

Presented by Ōtomo Tabito:

A Japanese harp of Paulownia wood

> fashioned from the youngest branches
> of a tree growing on Yūshi Mountain
> on the island of Tsushima

This harp appeared to me in a dream, assuming the form of a young girl and saying, "Once I extended my roots into a lofty peak on a distant island, and bleached my trunk in the splendid gleam of the orb. Long was I enveloped in fog, my heart playing among the mountains and rivers. In the distance I gazed upon wind and waves, as I hovered between use and uselessness—the tree spared for its height and the goose killed for its silence.[12] My only fear was that after my century of life I would rot in the bottom of some ravine. But it was my unexpected fortune to fall into the hands of an excellent craftsman. I was stripped apart and fashioned into a small harp. Though I know mine is but a tiny sound of rough quality, yet I hope somehow that I

---

[12] In *Chuang Tzu*, a tall tree is spared by a woodcutter because it is too large to use, and a goose is killed by its master because its silence makes it useless. A disciple observes that one is saved and the other is destroyed because of its uselessness, and Chuang Tzu remarks that it is best to stay between use and uselessness.

might become the beloved harp always kept by a fine gentle-
man at his side." Then she sang:

I wonder when,
and on which day
I will find for my pillow
the knees of one
who understands my song.

I recited a poem in response:

Though you are wood,
           and cannot speak,
surely you will be the harp
beloved of the hands
           of a splendid lord.

The harp maiden answered, "Humbly I receive your gra-
cious words. They give me great delight."
Finally I awoke. Profoundly moved by the words the
maiden had spoken in my dream, I could not remain silent.
So I have given this to a public messenger, and offer it for
your inspection.

The tenth month, seventh day, of the first year of
Tempyō
Presented, with deep respect, by messenger
to His Excellency Fujiwara Fusasaki,
the Illustrious General of the Central Guards[13]

---

[13] In the original this is followed by the characters 謹空, indicating a space
left open at the end of the letter as a mark of respect.

812

It is with profound delight that I humbly receive your gracious words, and know that my miserable existence has richly benefitted from your noble kindness. My special thoughts of you, longing to see you again, increase a hundred-fold more than ever. In a humble attempt to respond to your magnificent work, coming to me from beyond the white clouds' distance, I present you my clumsy effort at poetry. Submitted, with deep humility, by Fusasaki

Though it is wood,
    and cannot speak,
could I ever leave
my man's beloved harp
lying on the ground?

Submitted, with respect, to your Secretary
The eleventh month, eighth day
Attached as a message with the Captain
of the Dazaifu on his return

813 and 814

Poem by Yamanoue Okura about the heart-calming stones

    with tanka

Preface

On the fields of Kofu, in Fukae Village, Ito County, in the province of Chikuzen, there is a hill facing the sea, and on it are two stones. The larger stone is one foot, three inches, in length and one foot, ten inches, in circumference, weighing twenty-four pounds. The smaller stone is one foot, one inch, in length and one foot, nine inches, in circumference, weighing twenty-one pounds. Both stones are oval, shaped like chicken eggs. Their beauty is beyond description. These are the so-called "foot-long gems" (another version states that these are the two stones of Hirashiki in Sono County, in the province of Bizen). They are situated close by the roadside, just forty-nine miles from the horse station at Fukae. None who pass by, on public or private business, fail to dismount and genuflect before these stones. The elders have recounted through the ages, "When, in ancient times, the Empress Jingō set out on her expedition to conquer Silla, she picked up these stones and calmed her heart by placing them between her sleeves." (actually it was between the hems of her robe) "Therefore passersby pay homage to these stones." I have composed a poem about them:

It is an awesome thing
	to put into words:
at the time when Tarashihime,
			Divine Princess,
pacified the Korean kingdoms
she picked up this pair of stones
			like true gems
and prayed with them
so that she might calm
	her imperial heart.
She showed them
			to the people of the world
and, that they might be recounted
			through ten thousand ages,
with her own noble hands
she placed them
on the fields of Kofu

overlooking the depths of the sea,
    the fathomless cove of Fukae.
Very gods they are,
    shapes of divine will,
mysterious spirits before me now—
    noble and sacred!

814

Envoy

"Speak of me as long
as heaven and earth endure!"
So the mysterious spirit
took these as a shrine.

> The man who recounted the above
> matters to me was Takebe Ushimaro,
> an inhabitant of Mino Island, Ichi
> Village, in Naka County.

815-846

Thirty-two poems on the plum blossoms

Preface

    On the thirteenth day of the New Year, Tempyō 2 (730), a banquet was held at the estate of the venerable Ōtomo Tabito, Commander of the Dazaifu. The time was spring's splendid first month.[14] The air was clear, the wind was soft. The plum blossoms opened like a spray of powder before a dressing mirror, and the orchids gave off a fragrance as from a purse of perfume. Not only that, but clouds shifted over the dawn peaks, and the pines were covered with a

---

[14] The first month of the lunar calendar, corresponding to February.

fine silk as they trailed their canopies. Fog thickened in the mountain hollows, and birds trapped in its silky crepe wandered lost in the woods. In the garden were butterflies fluttering anew, and in the sky were geese from the old year returning north. Here we were, with the sky our canopy and the earth our seat, knee to knee, our wine cups flying back and forth. We were all together, and our harmony was such that we forgot the need for speech. Facing the clouds and mist that stretched out beyond us, we all opened our collars, each acting serenely as his heart desired, each taking a delighted fulfilment in his own thoughts. How could we express these emotions other than in the garden of writing? In Chinese poetry are recorded works on the falling plum blossoms. What difference between ancient and modern times? Come, let us too fashion a few small verses singing of the plum blossoms in the garden.

815

The first month is turned,
and spring is come;
let us take our pleasure
                    to the limit
as we greet the plum blossoms.

> *By Lord Ki, Vice-Commander of*
> *the Dazaifu*

816

I would have the plum flowers
always in my garden,
              never falling,
like the ones
      that bloom before me now.

> By Ono Oyu, Deputy Vice-Commander
> of the Dazaifu

817

In the garden
where the plum has blossomed,
have not green willows grown
so lush to make a canopy?

> By Awata Hitokami, Deputy Vice-
> Commander of the Dazaifu

818

Plum blossoms by my house,
first to bloom
              when spring arrives:
will I be watching them alone
as this spring day yields to dusk?

> By Yamanoue Okura, Governor of Chikuzen

819

This world of the alive
is thick with longing!
If so it must be,
then let me become a plum blossom.

> By Ōtomo,[15] *Governor of Bungo*

820

Now the plums are in full flower.
Take them for your garlands,
you comrades of the heart.
Now they are in full flower.

> *By Fujii Ōnari, Governor of Chikugo*

821

Pluck your garlands
from green willows
and plum blossoms.
Then drink! It does not matter
if afterwards they fall.

> *By the Priest Kasa (Mansei)*

---

[15] Which Ōtomo is unclear. One possibility is Ōtomo Miyori.

822

Plum blossoms fall
and scatter in my garden;
is this snow come streaming
from the distant heavens?

By the host, Ōtomo Tabito

823

Where do plum blossoms scatter?
So you wonder,
while here on Ki Mountain
the snow goes on falling.

By Ōtomo Momoyo, Captain of the Dazaifu

824

Mourning the plum blossoms' fall,
the nightingale cries
in the bamboo grove in my garden.

By Abe Okishima, Lieutenant of the Dazaifu

825

Let us disport
this day through to dusk,
taking our garlands

from green willow sprays
in the garden
where the plum has blossomed.

By Hanishi Momomura

826

How can I judge between them,
the spring willow swaying
and the plum blossoms by my house?

By the Scribe Shi[16] Ōhara

827

Spring comes, and the nightingale
cries hidden in the treetops
as it swoops
     to the lower sprays of plum.

By the Deputy Scribe Yamaguchi Wakamaro

828

However much we play,
each plucking a spray
    for his garland,

---

[16] A Japanese surname written in a Chinese monosyllabic style. I have reconstructed the Japanese surname (as in "Abe Okishima," author of poem no. 824) only when identification is historically certain. When, as in many of these cases, the single syllable could be an abbreviation from any of a number of Japanese surnames, I have left it as is (Shi 史, Tan 丹, etc.).

the lovely plum blossoms
delight us all the more.

        By the Judicial Administrator Tan Maro

829

Now that the plum
has bloomed and fallen,
is it not time for the cherry
to blossom in its turn?

        By the Pharmacist Chō Fukushi

830

Ten thousand generations may pass,
but the plum flower
shall go on blooming without cease.

        *By Saeki Ko'obito, Assistant Governor of
Chikuzen*

831

Spring is here
and yes, O plum,
you have blossomed—
the thought of you
robs me nightly of my sleep!

        By Itamochi Yasumaro, Governor of Iki

832

This entire day
will bring delight to all
who have picked their garlands
                from plum blossoms.

By the Shintō Priest Kō Inajiki

833

Each year,
when spring arrives,
let us take plum blossoms
            for our garlands
and delight ourselves with drink.

By the Judicial Scribe Ya Sukunamaro

834

The plum
        is now in full flower;
it seems that spring is here,
        sweet with the cries
        of a hundred birds.

By the Deputy Judicial Scribe Den Umahito

835

Plum blossoms
I had hoped to meet
with spring's arrival—
at today's party
we have come face to face.

        By the Pharmacist Kō Gitsū

836

The day we play
and never tire of it,
        our hands picking
        sprays of plum for garlands—
it is this day.

        By the Yin-Yang Master Isobe Norimaro

837

As if to tame the nightingale
crying over spring fields,
the plum flowers blossom
in the garden by my house.

        By the Secretary of Calculation Shiki Ōmichi

838

How the nightingale cries
by hills where plum blossoms
whirl from the trees—
as time turns to spring.

> *By Ka Hachimaro, Deputy Administrator of*
> *Ōsumi*

839

Men see mists rise and spread,
and snowfall on the fields of spring—
so thick do plum blossoms scatter.

> *By Den Makami, Deputy Administrator of*
> *Chikuzen*

840

Who took the plum blossoms
I picked for our canopy,
   our spring willow canopy,[17]
and set them floating
on the brim of our wine cups?

> *By Son Ochikata, Deputy Administrator of Iki*

---

[17] "Spring willow" seems to be a *formal* prelude for "canopy." The canopy itself is made up of plum blossoms.

841

As I hear the nightingale's cry,
I can see the plum flowers
blossom and fall
in the garden by my house.

By Kō Oyu, Deputy Administrator of Tsushima

842

How the nightingale
cries as it disports
among the lower branches
of the plum tree by my house—
mourning the blossoms about to fall.

By Kō Ama, Deputy Administrator of Satsuma

843

As I watch how all here play,
    picking plum blossoms
        for their garlands,
my mind turns to the capital.

By Hanishi Mimichi

844

O plum blossoms
whirling so wildly
that my eyes wonder
if snow is falling
by my woman's house!

> *By Ono Kunikata*

845

O plum blossoms
that the nightingale
waited for impatiently,
stay there unfalling
for that little one
who thinks of you.

> *By Kadobe Isotari, Deputy Administrator of*
> *Chikuzen*

846

All through the long spring day
    with its rising mists
we may pick them for garlands,
yet they are ever more precious—
    the plum blossoms!

> *By Ono Tamori*

847 and 848

Two additional poems, apart from the above collection but sent with it to Nara, expressing thoughts of the native city

The years of my flourishing
have faded in dreadful distance.
Even if I drank of the Elixir
    that lets you soar
    through the clouds
how could I hope to regain my youth?

Even more than a drink of the Elixir
    that lets you soar
    through the clouds
a glimpse of the capital would restore
this miserable man his youth.

849-852

Four poems, added later, responding to the plum blossom poems

849

O plum that blossoms
amid the remaining snow,
do not fall in haste,
even if that snow should melt.

850

The plum flourishes now,
its bloom is pillaging
the white from the snow.
Oh for someone to see it!

851

The plum blossoms
in full flourish
   by my house
are about to fall.
Oh for someone to see it!

852

The plum flower
spoke to me in a dream:
"I am a courtly blossom.
I pray you, float me in wine."

853

Preface: An excursion to the Matsura River

On a journey in Matsura, wandering here and there, I
happened to be taking in the sight of the pools of the
Tamashima River, when I came upon some maidens fish-
ing. Their blossom-like faces were of unparalleled beauty,
and the brilliant figure they made was beyond compare. It
was as if willow leaves opened in their brows, and peach
flowers bloomed in their cheeks. Their disposition was
more august than the very clouds, and their courtly elegance
without equal in this world.

I asked them, "Whose children are you, what village, what house? Or could you be goddesses?" The maidens all laughed and answered, "We are children of a house of fishermen, lowly people who live in straw huts. We have no village, and nothing that could be called a house. We have grown up constantly by the waterside, with our hearts delighting in the mountains. At times we would gaze upon the Lo River inlets, admiring with vain envy the beautiful fish. At other times we would lie in the Wu Gorge,[18] vacantly staring at the clouds and mists. And now we have met you, an illustrious guest, and in our excitement have told you everything in our hearts. How could you not wed us, and grow old together with us?"

"All right," I answered, "I humbly accept your command." But just at this time the sun was sinking below the western mountains, and the black steed I was riding stirred to depart.

Finally I wrote my feelings into this poem, which I am sending you. My poem:

Though people say
    they are daughters
        of angling fishermen,
one glance at them and I know
they are maidens of a good house.

854

A poem in response

Up this Tamashima River
    lie our houses,

---

[18] The Lo River and the Wu Gorge both appear in *The Dwelling of Playful Goddesses*. Nakanishi Susumu also suggests the "*Fu* of the Lo Goddesses," a work which was popular at the time, as a possible inspiration.

but we are too ashamed of them,
                    my Lord,
to show you where.

855-857

*Three poems in further response to the maidens, by us
ignoble travellers*

855

The shallows glisten
in the Matsura River,
and as you stand in them, my woman,
        angling the sweetfish,
you have wet the hems of your robe.

856

You girls who stand
    angling the sweetfish
in the Tamashima River
        in Matsura—
Oh I do not know
the way to your home!

857

Women who angle young sweetfish
in the streams of Matsura,
        where men from distant lands
                are awaited—
let me be the one
pillowed in their arms!

858-860

Three more poems by the maidens in response

858

If my love were merely level
like the waves in the Matsura stream,
    where we angle young sweetfish,
would I long for you like this?

859

When spring comes
the young sweetfish run
in the narrows of the stream
    by my native village—
impatiently awaiting you.

860

Even if the seven shallows
of the Matsura River stagnate,
still I shall wait for you,
my love never stagnant.

861-863

Poems added by someone later

> By Ōtomo Tabito, the venerable
> Commander of the Dazaifu

861

Swift are the shallows
in the Matsura stream:
do they wet the hems
of their crimson robes
as they angle the sweetfish?

862

Must I go on longing,
never to see
        the Tamashima River
        in Matsura
that everybody sees?

863

How I envy the one
there watching the women
who angle young sweetfish
in the Matsura River,
in the Tamashima bends!

864 and 865

From Yoshida Yoroshi

Humbly I received your letter of the fourth month, sixth
day. On bended knee I opened the letter box and read your
noble words. My spirit brightened, like T'ai Ch'u's with
the moon in his breast pocket.[19] My trivial cares vanished,

---

[19] The *Shih Shuo Shin Yü* mentions T'ai Chu as having "such a cheerful
personality that it seems he has the sun and moon in his breast." Most of
Yoroshi's letter is written in Chinese clichés.

making me feel as if I were looking at Le Kuang—as if gazing at the heavens.[20]

It seems that, as you journey to the distant frontiers, your heart is pained with thoughts of the time that was, the months and years that do not stand still for us, and that memories of youth bring tears to your eyes. But remember, the master mind is calm in the face of shifting circumstances, and the superior man is free from discontent. I entreat you, Lord, to spread virtue like Lu Kung, who tamed the pheasant in the morning, and to leave behind benevolent acts like K'ung Yu, who freed the turtle in the evening[21]—so that your name may be spoken of, like Chang Ch'ang's and Chao Kuang Han's,[22] a hundred generations hence, so that your life, like Chih Sung Tzu's and Wang Tzu Ch'iao's,[23] may extend a thousand years.

And the works I received with your letter—the beautiful words recited by the assembled talents at the noble banquet in your plum garden, your dialog with the goddesses by the gemlike pools of the Matsura River—they belong with the dialogs of Confucius and his disciples, when each spoke on the apricot terrace, they are of a kind with Ts'ao Chih's "*Fu* of the Goddesses," in which he released his carriage steeds into the marsh of fragrant grasses by the Lo River. With gratitude and joy I read them over and over again, and recited them aloud. The sincerity of my longing for you, O Lord, is greater than that of a dog or horse for its master. The feelings with which I revere your virtue are like the sunflower's as it gazes upward to the sun. More-

[20] The *Chin Shu* mentions Le Kuang as being so cheerful that looking at him was "like sweeping away the clouds and mist and gazing at the blue expanse of the heavens."

[21] Lu Kung's deed appears in the *Hou Han Shu*, Le Kuang's in the *Chin Shu*.

[22] Chang Ch'ang and Chao Kuang Han were both famous officials during the Han Dynasty.

[23] Chih Sung Tzu, of the legendary Shen Nung age, and Wang Tzu Ch'iao, a prince of the Chou Dynasty, were famous as hermit immortals.

over, we are separated by the blue sea's expanse, with the white-clouded heavens between us; in vain gathers my yearning for you, with neck outstretched. How can I assuage this anxiety?

It is now the beginning of autumn. I humbly pray that all of Heaven's providence be upon you, renewed from day to day.

I submit this letter with the bearers who brought the *Sumo* wrestlers, on their return to Kyushu.

> *With deep respect,*
> *Yoroshi*

864

A poem presented in response to the poems by the various people on the plum blossoms

Rather than being left behind
and all this time longing
   to be with you,
I wish I could be a plum blossom
growing in your garden.

865

A poem in response to your poems about the goddesses of Matsura

Could the maidens
by the coves of Matsura—
land that awaits you—
be fishergirls
from the land of eternity?

866 and 867

Two more poems I wrote as I kept on thinking of you

I think of it afar, afar:
the land of Tsukushi
separated from me
by a thousand-fold of white clouds.

You are gone,
and the days have turned long;
the trees that stand in your garden
        on the Nara Road
have wizened with age.

868-870

Submitted by Okura with the greatest humility:

   I, Okura, understand that the Commander of the Dazaifu and the Governors of the various provinces, in accordance with practice established by law, do go among their jurisdictions to observe the various customs within. This fills my heart with various emotions, but it is a difficult task to express them in words. Therefore I respectfully submit to you three lowly poems I have written, by which I hope to discharge the feelings coiled inside me. The poems:

868

Will I only know it
by the sound of its name,
the mountain
where Princess Sayo of Matsura
        waved her scarf?

869

Who has seen the rock
where stood Tarashihime,
        divine Empress,
that she might fish?[24]

870

The road to Matsura
does not take a hundred days;
I could go there today
and be back tomorrow.
What, then, hinders me?

871

   The youth Ōtomo Sadehiko received the favor of a spe-
cial imperial command ordering him to serve as messenger
to the outer provinces. He readied his ship, then set out
into the rising waves. His lover, Princess Sayo of Matsura,
sighed over the ease with which fate had taken him away,
and lamented the difficulty of ever seeing him again. She
climbed to the summit of a tall mountain and watched his
ship fade into the distance. Her heart was broken with
sorrow, and her soul was choked with darkness. At last she
removed the scarf from around her neck and waved it at
him. None of those who stood beside her watching could
keep from crying. Therefore this mountain is named *Hire-
furu-mine*, Scarf Waving Peak. I have written a poem
about it:

   [24] This refers to a legend in the *Kojiki* which records Tarashihime (Empress
Jingū) fishing for sweetfish in the river in Matsura on her way to conquer
Korea. A variant on this poem has "that she might angle sweetfish" for the
line "that she might fish."

Born from the scarf
that Princess Sayo,
yearning for her husband,
waved in Matsura—
where distant men are awaited—
O mountain's name!

872

Poem added by someone later

Was it so the mountain's name
would speak her deed to later ages
that Princess Sayo waved her scarf
upon this mountain?

873

Poem added by someone after that

O Princess Sayo of Matsura
who waved her scarf, it seems,
from this mountain peak
so that her deed would be recounted
for ten thousand generations.

874 and 875

Two poems added by someone else after that

O Princess Sayo of Matsura
who must have waved her scarf
to tell the ship sailing on the offing
of the plain of waters
to return.

O Princess Sayo of Matsura,
how she must have loved him—
waving her scarf
to stop a sailing ship!

876-879

*Four Japanese poems written on the day a farewell party
was held for Ōtomo Tabito at the Dazaifu Library*

876

Would I were a bird
that soars the skies!
I would see you all the way
            to the capital
and fly back home.

877

You leave us all
dejected and forlorn,
but will you not forget us
when your steed approaches
Tatsuta Mountain?

878

Though we speak of sorrow,
only later will we truly know it;
how could our desolation be complete
before you, O Lord, are gone?

879

Go now, O Lord,
and take your charge
of the realm under heaven
for ten thousand generations,
never leaving the Court.

880-882

Three poems expressing personal feelings on the occasion

880

Five years of living
in this rustic land
at the far reaches
        of the heavens
have made me forget
        the city ways.

881

Will I go on
forever sighing like this,
unmindful of the borders
                of the years
as they come and go?

882

Have sympathy, O my master,
and when spring comes call me
to the capital at Nara.

883

*A poem written later by Prince Mishima in response to
the poems about Princess Sayo of Matsura*

I have heard of it,
but my eyes have yet to see it,
the mountain in Matsura—
land that awaits you—
where they say Princess Sayo
          waved her scarf.

884 and 885

Two poems of Ōtomo Kumakori

      written for him by the Scribe Asada
      Yasu

Here on the long road
far from my homeland,
is my life to pass away
this soul-darkening day,
no words spoken with my parents?

My life fades easily
as the morning dew.
I cannot yield it
in a strange land!
I long for my parents' eyes.

886 and 891

Six poems respectfully presented in response to Asada Yasu's, expressing Kumakori's intention for him

> *By Yamanoue Okura, the Governor of Chikuzen*

Preface

Ōtomo Kumakori was a man of Mashiki County in the province of Higo. At the age of eighteen, on the seventeenth day of the sixth month of the third year of Tempyō (731), he became a retainer in the service of the governor of that province, who had been appointed Bearer of the *Sumō* Wrestlers, and set off for the capital. But—could it have been Heaven's will?—unfortunately he contracted a disease on the road, and died at the Takaba horse station in Saeki County in the province of Aki.

Just before his death Kumakori gave a long sigh and said, "I have heard it recounted that, 'Man's body, a temporary assemblage of the elements, is easily destroyed, and the course of life, like bubbles on the water, is hard to hold back.' Thus the thousand saints have all passed away, and the hundred sages could not remain in this world. How, then, could a mere common man like myself, of mean station, possibly escape from death? But I am concerned about my aged parents, both of them alive in their humble hut, who pass their days waiting for my return. Naturally their hearts will be rent with grief. If I do not return when they expect me to, I know their tears will be enough to blind them. O my father, how sorrowful for you! O my mother, how painful for you! It does not bother me that I myself must tread the road of death. I only lament the hardships my parents will face when they are left behind without me. Today we must part for eternity—in what life will we ever meet again?"

Kumakori then composed six poems, and died. The poems:

886

To go up to the palace
        swept with sunlight,
I left my mother's arms,
        my mother
        with her milk-full breasts,
and set out for the depths
of lands I have never known,
and crossed beyond
a hundred folds of mountains.
Talking with my companions
and wondering how soon
I could set my eyes
        on the capital—
then pain struck my body,
I collapsed
on a corner of the road—
road like a jewelled spear—
and, plucking grass
and spreading gromwell
        for my bed,
I lay down,
and as I lay
        I sighed with longing:
If I were in my homeland,
my father would hold and nurse me;
if I were in my house,
my mother would hold and nurse me.
The world, it seems,
        comes but to this—
must I end my life
falling by the roadside
        like a dog?

887

In which direction will I leave,
my soul darkened,
parting from my mother,
    with her milk-full breasts,
unable to meet her eyes?

888

How can I make my way
through the darkness
down the long road
I have never known?
I have no provisions.

889

If I were home
and my mother held
    and nursed me,
it would soothe my heart,
even—if I must—
    were I to die.

890

O my father and mother
who must be waiting for me,
counting the days
since I went away
and thinking, "Today! Today!"

891

Must I depart for eternity,
leaving behind
my father and mother,
whom I can never see
twice in a single lifetime?[25]

892

Dialog of the Destitute

with tanka

"On nights when rain falls,
            mixed with wind,
on nights when snow falls,
            mixed with rain,
I am cold.
And the cold
      leaves me helpless:
I lick black lumps of salt
and suck up melted dregs of *sake*.
Coughing and sniffling,
I smooth my uncertain wisps
                  of beard.
I am proud—
      I know no man
            is better than me.
But I am cold.
I pull up my hempen nightclothes
and throw on every scrap

---

[25] If read literally, this poem seems redundant. But "whom I can never see / twice in a single lifetime" is a quasi-epithetical modification of "my father and mother," operating like a formal (i.e., non-semantic) "pillow-word."

of cloth shirt that I own.
But the night is cold.
And I wonder how a man like you,
  even poorer than myself,
with his father and mother
starving and freezing,
with his wife and children
begging and begging
  through their tears,
can get through the world alive
  at times like this."

"Wide, they say,
  are heaven and earth—
but have they shrunk for me?
Bright, they say,
  are the sun and moon—
but do they refuse to shine for me?
Is it thus for all men,
  or for me alone?
Above all, I was born human,
I too toil for my keep—
as much as the next man—
yet on my shoulders hangs
a cloth shirt
not even lined with cotton,
these tattered rags
thin as strips of seaweed.
In my groveling hut,
 my tilting hut,
sleeping on straw
cut and spread right on the ground,
with my father and mother
  huddled at my pillow

and my wife and children
    huddled at my feet,
I grieve and lament.
Not a spark rises in the stove,
and in the pot
a spider has drawn its web.
I have forgotten
what it is to cook rice!
As I lie here,
a thin cry tearing from my throat—
       a tiger thrush's moan—
then, as they say,
to slice the ends
of a thing already too short,
to our rough bed
comes the scream of the village headman
     with his tax collecting whip.
Is it so helpless and desperate,
the way of life in this world?"

893

Envoy

I find this world
a hard and shameful place.
But I cannot fly away—
I am not a bird.

> *Presented by Yamanoue Okura with profound
> humility*

894

Poem wishing Godspeed to the Ambassador to China

with two envoys

It has been recounted
down through time
since the age of the gods:
that this land of Yamato
is a land of imperial deities'
         stern majesty,
a land blessed by the spirit of words.
Every man of the present
sees it before his eyes
and knows it to be true.

Men fill this land
with their numbers,
but among them our Emperor,
sovereign of the high-shining sun,
a very god,
in the fullness of his love,
chose for this mission
you, the son of a house
that governs the realm under heaven.
And with the favor
of his great command,
you have been sent
to the distant borders of China.

As you set out,
all the mighty deities
that, in their godliness, abide
by the shore and by the offing,
there to rule the plain of waters,

lead you by the prow of your ship.
And the mighty gods
      of heaven and earth,
first among them
the Supreme Spirit of the Land
            of Yamato,
soar from the distant heavenly skies
      to watch over you.

And on the day when,
your mission accomplished,
      you return,
again the mighty gods
shall take the prow of your ship
      in their noble hands
and bring you straight
as a black rope stretched
from Chika Cape
to your berth by Ōtomo's noble beach.
Go without hindrance,
go with good fortune,
and quickly return!

895 and 896

Envoys

I shall sweep the beach clean
by the field of pines
at Ōtomo's noble cove,
and stand there waiting for you.
Quickly return!

When I hear the news
that the imperial craft
has berthed at Naniwa Cove,
I shall run to greet you,
my waistcord trailing loose.

On the third month, first day, of the fifth year of
Tempyō, you visited me at my home. I present
you this on the third.
From Yamanoue Okura, with humility
To His Excellency the Ambassador to China

An essay lamenting his own long illness

By Yamanoue Okura

In my private thoughts it occurs to me that even those men who obtain their livelihood by hunting, morning and evening, on the mountains and the plains are able to make their way through life without calamity (I speak of those who, with bow and arrow in their hands, ignoring the six fasting days on which the taking of life is forbidden, slay every animal they come across, regardless of young or old, pregnant or not). Even those who fish day and night in the rivers and on the sea are vouchsafed their fortune and their safe passage through life (I speak of the fisherman and the diving woman, each with his or her effort of work, the man clutching his bamboo pole who angles skillfully over the waves, the woman, with scythe and basket tied to her waist, who dives into the sea to pluck life from the depths).

But I, since the day I was born until today, have intended to do only good deeds and have had no thoughts of doing evil (I have followed the teachings "to eschew the various evil deeds" and "to perform the various good deeds"). I have reverenced the Three Treasures—Buddha, Law, and Priesthood—, foregoing not a day of effort (reading the sutras every day and atoning for my sins). I have venerated the myriad deities, neglecting not an evening (doing homage to the various deities of heaven and earth). Oh how shameful! What crime have I committed, that I should meet with this dreadful disease! (Is this for past crimes, or is it the result of present transgressions? How could I, who am innocent of sin, be struck down with this illness?)

Many are the months and years since I first contracted this disease (it has been more than ten years). I am presently seventy-four years old. My hair is spotted with white, and my muscles have lost their strength. And now to the sufferings of old age, now to those burdens has been added this affliction of sickness. This is what the proverbs must mean when they speak of pouring salt into a painful wound, of cutting off the edges of a stick already too short. I cannot move my four limbs, my hundred joints all ache, my body feels terribly heavy, as if I were carrying a load of a hundred and fifty pounds.[26] Clutching a strip of cloth, I try to pull myself up, only to collapse like a bird with broken wings. Leaning on my cane and trying to walk, I am like an old donkey whose legs are gone.

My body is sunk deeply in the vulgar, and my heart is tainted with the dirt of this world. Therefore I wished to know where affliction lurks and where the curse of retribution is hidden. I went to inquire at every sorcerer's gate, to every shaman's chamber. Whether true or false, I followed all their instructions, never failing to hang prayer cloths and offer invocations. But the pangs of disease only

---

[26] The original text has "*kinseki*" (鈞石), a curious combination of two different weights. This is followed by an interlinear note which, going through the various weight equivalents in use at the time, concludes, "four *kin* (鈞) equal one *jaku* (石), all together 120 *kon* (斤)." This would be 158.4 pounds.

increased all the more, and showed not the slightest abatement.

I have heard that in previous ages there were many excellent doctors who could cure the ailments of all men. When it came to the likes of Yü Fu, Pien Ch'ueh, Hua T'o, Ho Huan of Ch'in, Ke Chih-ch'uan, T'ao the Hermit and Chang Chung-ching, all were excellent physicians living in this world, and there was no disease they could not cure (Pien Ch'ueh's *sheng* was Ch'in, his *tzu* was Yueh Jen. He was a man of Po Hai County. He would open the patient's breast, remove the heart and replace it in a new position, then apply a divine elixir. When the patient awoke, he would be completely recovered to his normal state.

(Hua To's *tzu* was Yuan Hua. He was a man of Ch'iao in the land of P'ei. When disease accumulated deep in the inner organs, he would cut the patient open at the intestines, remove the affliction, suture him and dress the wound with an ointment. In four to five days the patient would be cured).

Though I search for great physicians like these, it is impossible to find them. If I should come across a sagely doctor and divine medicine, I would beg the doctor to split open my five inner organs, reach into the innermost crevices of my *kao* and *huang* (The *huang* is the diaphragm, the area below the heart. It is beyond treatment. Neither medicine nor the acupuncturist's needle have any effect on it), and expose in their hiding place the inner twins of disease[27] (Duke Ching of Chin contracted an illness. Huan, a physician of Ch'in, examined him and went back home, saying it was a demon that was killing the Duke).

When the liferoot is exhausted and the span of years determined by heaven is at its end, it is still a sorrowful

---

[27] This conception of illness appears in the *Tzo Chuan*.

thing to be afflicted with illness (of saints and sages, and all things enspirited with life, who among them can escape this path?). How much more so when one must face this demon's onslaught before reaching half of life's allotted length, racked with sudden sickness while one's complexion is still flush and in its prime! Which of the great hardships lurking in the world could be more terrible than this? (The *Chih Pu Chi* states, "Hsü Hsüan-fang of Pei Hai, former Governor of Kuang P'ing, had a daughter who died at the age of eighteen. Her ghost appeared to P'ing Ma Tzu and said, 'I estimate my allotted lifespan to have been more than eighty years. Already four years have passed since I fell victim to the murderous demon.' Because she told this to P'ing Ma Tzu, she was able to return to life." In the sutras it is written, "The longevity of those in the human realm is one hundred and twenty years." If I may add my own thoughts, it seems to me that this number does not necessarily exclude a greater one. So that in the *Sutra of Longevity Extended* we read, "There was a priest by the name of Nantatsu. When he approached his end, he petitioned the Buddha for greater longevity, and his life was extended for eighteen years." But those who thoroughly dedicate themselves can exist as long as heaven and earth. Ripe old age or untimely death—these are the rewards of one's own deeds. Life's length may be even cut in half. And one may succumb without even attaining that number— thus life which is "less than half." Jen Cheng Chün tells us, "Sickness enters from the mouth. Therefore a superior man regulates his food and drink." According to this, man does not necessarily contract disease from demons.

(Now then, first, the excellent theories of the many physicians; second, the noble commandment to refrain from too much food and drink; and third, man's desires, which make it difficult for him to put his understanding of the first two into practice—these three things have long been familiar to us, filling our eyes and plenishing our ears. Pao Pu Tzu states, "The only reason a man does not grieve is because he has not been told the day of his death. If he knew he could extend his life by having his nose and feet chopped off, he would go right ahead and do it."

(My examination of these texts convinces me that my illness is the direct result of the food and drink I intake, and that there is no way I can cure myself).

In *The Shorter Expositions of Duke Po* it is written, "Longevity, I think, can be attained through one's own efforts. Life is to be craved, death to be feared." Life is the greatest virtue between heaven and earth. Therefore a dead man is less than a living rat. Though a man may be a king or a prince, and accumulate a mountain of gold, a single day after he has breathed his last no one calls him rich. Though his power may extend vast as the ocean, no one considers him noble anymore. *The Dwelling of Playful Goddesses* tells us, "People beneath the Nine Springs of Hades are not worth a penny." Confucius states, "That which we receive from heaven and cannot change is form. That which we receive by heaven's will and cannot increase is the span of life." (This appears in *Doctor Kuei Ku's Book of Fortunes*.)

Thus we know that life is extremely noble, that to be alive is a most precious thing. I want to speak of it, but my words fail me. How shall I speak of it? I want to consider it, but my thoughts fall short. How shall I consider it? This, it seems, is the common lament of the wise man and the fool, of all men ancient and modern. The months and years race away, day and night know no rest (Huei Tzu states, "That which departs never to return is the years." This is what Confucius sighed at by the river). Old age and disease lure each other out, and assault us in the morning and the evening. While the pleasures of a lifetime remain unexhausted before my eyes (in Emperor Wen of Wei's poem of lament for Shih Hsien is written, "Before the evening's pleasures are over in the Western Garden, already you are dust in the Northern Cemetery"), a thousand years of painful sorrow are already waiting at my back (an ancient poem says, "Man's life does not fill a century—how can one sorrow for the thousand years after?").

Each living thing longs in its mortal body for immortal life. Thus Taoist monks enter of their own accord into famous mountains with books on holy medicine strapped to their backs, and alchemists cultivate their bodies and calm their souls in their quest for longevity. Pao Pu Tzu records King Shen Nung's words, "How can one attain a long life with all one's illnesses uncured?" Duke Po also states, "Life is a good thing, death an evil thing." If, unfortunately, one is unable to attain a great age, one should still count it a considerable blessing to get through life without illness. I am now afflicted with a disease that leaves me unable to sleep or rise. Turning to the east, turning to the west, I do not know what to do. All the most dreadful misfortunes have fallen upon me.

They say heaven heeds the entreaties of men. If it be true, then, begging the skies, I implore heaven to quickly take this sickness away and restore me to my normal state!

—How shameful of me to use a rat as an example! (it appears above)

A poem of sorrow and lament for life in this world—the body a temporary coming together of elements that soon disintegrates, existence that easily vanishes and is hard to retain

Preface

In my private thoughts it occurs to me that the teachings of Sakyamuni and Maitreya spread enlightenment in the human realm by first expounding the Three Beliefs (belief in the Buddha, the Law and the Priesthood), then unfolding the Five Commandments (one, not to kill; two, not to steal; three, not to be promiscuous; four, not to lie; five, not to be inebrious). The injunctions handed down by the Duke of Chou and Confucius redeem the nation by first propounding the Three Bonds (lord and vassal, father and son, husband and wife), then establishing the Five Teachings (for the father to be righteous, for the mother to be compassionate, for the elder brother to be amicable, for the younger brother to be obedient, and for the son to be filial). Thus we know that, although men are led by two philosophies, the enlightenment to be obtained from them is one.

But in this world no substance is permanent. Thus hills yield to valleys and valleys change to hills. And the span of a man's life is not determined—thus the difference between longevity and untimely death. In the wink of an eye a hundred years of life are extinguished, in the bend of an elbow a thousand years are gone without a trace. In the morning one is host of a banquet table, in the evening the guest of Hades. Even a white steed's gallop cannot match the speed with which the Underworld overtakes us. On the green pine over the grave, in vain hangs the sword of loyalty; and in the fields the white wisteria simply sways in the sorrowful wind.[28]

By this we know, that this world has no hermitage where

[28] In a Chinese legend, recorded in the *Shih Chi*, Li K'ung wished to present a sword to Hsü Chun but, finding that he was already dead, hung the sword on the pine by his grave.

The wisteria was a feature of Chinese cemeteries and an image of death in Chinese poetry.

we can hide from death, that on the plain there is only the tower of eternal night.[29] The saints of early times have passed away, and the sages of later times could not remain in this world. If a man could buy his way out of this fate, who, even among the ancients, would not have paid the price in gold? I have never heard of a man who survived alone to witness the end of his age. Thus the elder Vimalakirti's jewelled body fell to pestilence in his priestly chamber, and Sakyamuni's golden form yielded to the shadows of the sal trees. The scriptures tell us, "If you desire not the Darkness to creep up behind you, let not the Angel of Virtue stand before you" (the Angel of Virtue is life, the Darkness is death). Therefore we know that all who are born must surely die. If one desires not death, it is best not to be born. Even if we could learn the numbers fated for life and death, how could we ever know the moment when existence passes into oblivion?

Changes in this life are as transitory
        as the wink of an eye,
and the passage of human events as short
        as the bend of an elbow.
In vain I drift through the great void
        like the floatng clouds,
both my mind and body exhausted,
        with nowhere to turn.

897-903

Seven poems about having disease added to my already aged body, the hardships of the years, and my longing for my children

    one chōka, six tanka

[29] A Chinese image of the tomb.

897

I wish my span
of soul-swollen life
("in the human realm," it is said,
"a hundred and twenty years")
to be peaceful
and safe from disturbance,
free of affliction
and free of mournful disaster.
But grief and hardship
are our lot in this world.
And as if, as they say,
to pour bitter salt
on a wound
already festering with pain,
as if, as they say,
to throw an extra burden
on a horse
already weighted down
with layer upon layer,
to my already aged body
is added the scourge of disease.
I lament through the days
         until dusk
and sigh through the nights
         until dawn.
Through long years
have I suffered with this sickness,
the months amass
with my painful moans.
"If it is to be like this,"
         I think,
"then let me die."
But it is not my right
to die,

and leave behind my children
who leap about me
like the flies of June.
As I gaze on them,
my heart smoulders with worry.
In my anguished thoughts
        of all these things,
I find myself weeping
        and crying aloud.

Envoys

898

Unable to assuage my heart,
I find myself—
like the birds that cry
as they soar hidden in the clouds—
weeping and crying aloud.

899

The pain leaves me helpless:
I want to leave,
                to run away,
but my children keep me back.

900

Oh cottons and silks of the rich,
more than can dress
their few children's bodies,
that they let rot and throw away!

901

Will I go on grieving like this,
not knowing what to do,
unable to dress my children
even in garments of rough cloth?

902

Fragile life,
like bubbles on the water:
I live with the prayer
that even it may be as long
as mulberry rope
a thousand armfuls' long.

903

My body is worthless,
like a wristband
    of plain Yamato pattern.
But how I desire it to last
    a thousand years!

> This last poem was written back in
> the second year of Jinki (725).
> However, it has been placed here
> because of its resemblance to the
> poem before it.

904-906

*Three poems by Yamanoue Okura, longing for his son
Furuhi*

one chōka and two tanka

904

The seven priceless gems
that men of this world
treasure and crave
mean nothing to me.
Furuhi,
the child born between us,
was like a fine white pearl.
In dawn bright
with the morning star
he never left our bedside
   where we slept
     under well-woven quilts.
Standing or sitting,
he would play with us.
When dusk came
with the evening star,
he would say,
  "Let's go to sleep,"
and take us by our hands
and urge us in his lovely way,
"Mother and father,
never leave my side.
Let me sleep between you
like the middle branch
of the lily's three."[30]

---

[30] The lily is one of several plants identified with the obscure *sakikusa*
(三枝), whose characters mean "triple-branched."

Then without warning
a blast of evil wind swept over us.
I did not know what to do.
Helplessly
I hung offering strands
        of white cloth
and, grasping a true clear mirror,
begging the skies, I implored
the gods of heaven.
Prostrate, I groveled
to the gods of earth.
On shaking feet I pleaded:
"Sick or hale—
it is by your whim, o gods!"
But not for a moment
        did he recover.
Time slowly
ravaged his features,
morning after morning
he spoke less and less
until his life,
    that swelled with spirit,
                stopped.
In frenzied grief
I leaped and danced,
I stamped and screamed,
I groveled to the earth
and glared at heaven,
I beat my breast and wailed.
I have let fly the child
I held in my hands.
This is the way of the world!

Envoys

905

He is young,
and does not know the way.
O Angel of Hades,
I shall send you an offering.
Carry him there on your back.

906

With offerings I implore you:
lead him directly
    without fail,
and show him the path
    to Heaven.

> The name of the author of the last
> poem is yet unknown. However,
> because of its resemblance to the
> other poems in style and to the rest
> of Yamanoue Okura's poetry in
> attitude, it has been placed here after
> the other two.

INDEX OF POETS

By Poem Numbers

Library of Congress Cataloging in Publication Data

Man'yōshū. English.
  The ten thousand leaves.

  (Princeton library of Asian translations)
  Includes index.
  1. Japanese poetry—To 794—Translations into
English.   2. English poetry—Translations from
Japanese.   I. Levy, Ian Hideo, 1950-   II. Title.
III. Series.
PL758.15.A3   1981   895.6'1'008   80-8561
ISBN 0-691-06452-0